presents

Stuff Dutch Moms Like

Copyright © 2016 by Colleen Geske

All rights reserved. No part of this publication may be reproduced, stored in a retrieval system, or transmitted, in any form or in any means—by electronic, mechanical, photocopying, recording or otherwise—without prior written permission.

Words by Colleen Geske

Editing by Tricia and Allan Geske

Production by Moses Faleafaga

Published in the Netherlands by Stuff Dutch People Like

Some of the material in this book may have originally appeared, in different form, on the popular blog StuffDutchPeopleLike.com

Photo & other credits can be found on page 216

ISBN 978-90-821336-4-6

Printed in the EU

10 9 8 7 6 5 4 3 2 1

www.stuffdutchpeoplelike.com
www.facebook.com/stuffdutchpeoplelike
www.instagram.com/stuffdutchpeoplelike
www.twitter.com/stuffdutchlike

For media inquiries, corporate & volume sales or any other request, please contact us at hello@stuffdutchpeoplelike.com

STUFF DUTCH MOMS LIKE

Contents

INTRODUCTION

I first arrived in Amsterdam on a cold and wet day in 2004. I had precisely three days to determine whether or not I was going to pack up my entire life in Canada, kiss my family and friends goodbye, and move to the lowlands for a two-year work contract. For three days straight the rain poured and the wind howled, yet somehow, stepping out of my hotel on that third day, I knew the decision had already been made. Amsterdam had stolen my heart and wasn't planning on giving it back anytime soon.

One month later, I was back in town with two massive suitcases, one pair of rose-tinted glasses, and endless questions. What was with the chocolate sprinkles? Did I have to do these elaborate air-kisses with everyone I met? Was I, in fact, incredibly short or were the Dutch simply giants? And, most importantly, would I ever be able to pronounce—let alone understand—the Dutch word *gezellig*?

Over the years, these questions were answered, but embarking on the adventure of motherhood in the Netherlands brought forth a whole slew of new ones. The Dutch midwifery system seemed far too casual. Home births were not urban legends, as I had hoped, but a frightening reality. Working mothers were expected to start working a mere three months after giving birth and breastfeeding rates were shockingly low. It seemed I had entered an entirely new phase of culture shock—and this time the cultural divide appeared much further apart than my initial experiences eight years prior. Could I actually give birth—let alone raise a child—in this country, far, far away from the comforts and familiarities of home?

With so many differences between North America and the Netherlands on the subjects of pregnancy, birth, and parenting, I found myself obsessing over which way was, in fact, the "right way." I spent countless hours researching and debating each side. Unfortunately, there were no black-and-white answers to be found, and the closer I observed Dutch mothers (and children), the more I began to realize that they were certainly not suffering as a result of some seemingly "backward" ways. Their births appeared more natural, their way of mothering more relaxed, and their children—albeit often running wild— seemed to be having a hell of a good time in the process. Were Dutch mothers able to have their cake and eat it too? I needed to know, so I embarked on a journey to find out the real stuff that Dutch mothers like—and how I could incorporate some of it into my own little Amsterdam life!

CHAPTER 1

PREGNANCY

Let me start by admitting that I was the foreigner who swore she would never give birth in the Netherlands. I was *that* expat (you know the one), who accused the Netherlands of disproportionately high infant-mortality rates, unsafe home-birth practices, and cruelly refusing drugs to labouring women for no apparent reason. You see, it wasn't entirely my fault, as these three alarming notions made up the standard set of urban legends in the new-to-the-Netherlands circle and the scared-shitless-to-have-a-baby-in-a-foreign-country. For those new to Dutch culture and already weary of its in-your-face directness and mysterious medical system (*what, paracetamol again??!*), it can be very hard to sort fact from fiction.

Discussions with other foreigners living in the Netherlands only served to solidify my growing fears. Everyone had a shocking statistic to share; or worse, a cautionary tale from some friend-of-a-friend who dared to give birth in the Netherlands and things, inevitably, had gone wrong. No one seemed to ever remember all the details from so-and-so's best friend's sister's cousin's birth experience, because what mattered most was the underlining message: it wasn't safe to give birth in the Netherlands. So think twice!

Of course, it was no surprise that, once pregnant, I wasn't exactly enthusiastic about the prospect of birthing here in the Lowlands. The above mentioned urban legends swirled through my mind, keeping me up at night trying to sort out the feasibility of an elaborate plan to give birth back home.

However, having been through the entire birth process (start to finish) not once, but twice in the Netherlands, I am happy to report that I'm now a convert.

In this chapter

- Affordable maternity care
- Midwives
- "No worries"
- *Gezellig* interiors
- Personalized care
- Round-the-clock attention
- Staying fit and active

A combination of sorting facts from fiction and firsthand experience led me to a much better understanding of this country's actual birth system.

What I did learn along the way was that the Dutch system *is* entirely different from any other country—but this difference is definitely not a bad thing and, in fact, I'd argue exactly the opposite. Don't believe me? Keep reading!

What makes pregnancy so different in the Netherlands? What do Dutch moms do differently during their pregnancy?

Affordable maternity care

One of the questions foreign mothers in the Netherlands often ask is, "How much does giving birth here actually cost?" At one of the first "pregnant meet-ups" I attended, a pregnant American mom had barely sat down on the chair next to me before she asked, in a panic, if anyone had been able to get the full scope on exactly *how* much it would set us back to give birth in a Dutch hospital. Coming from a country (Canada) with universal health care and paying a reasonable Dutch health contribution each month, I just assumed that it was part of the basic insurance package.

I had taken it completely for granted, as most Dutch women do, that being an expectant mother in the Netherlands meant not having to worry about the financial burden associated with such a fundamental human act.

Dutch women are afforded the (I think rightful) luxury of not having to consider, stress, or worry about the financial implications of becoming a mother. Almost all maternity costs are covered by the mandatory health insurance. This includes:

- obstetric care during pregnancy (midwife appointments/consults)

- obstetric care during childbirth (costs of a midwife, or gynaecologist/obstetrician)

- pregnancy ultrasounds (12 weeks and 20 weeks)

- the "non-invasive prenatal test" (NIPT)—this test was added in 2015 to the basic insurance, with the precondition of a positive 'combination test'

- cost of hospital stay (if a hospital birth is required on medical grounds)*

- after-care (*kraamzorg*)

Birth in a hospital without a medical indication does require a minimum personal contribution.

According to a recent report, the average total price charged for pregnancy and newborn care in the United States was between $30,000 – $50,000 with commercial insurers paying an average of $18,329 – $27,866. A further survey by Childbirth Connection found that American women with insurance pay out of pocket an average of $3,400 per birth. One does not want to imagine what the average cost would be for an American woman without insurance!

What do Dutch moms have to say about midwives?

Dutch mom

"I like being in touch with midwives rather than doctors, because it makes it more personal."

"Midwives make for a much less medicalized system. I like that very much. I do, however, think that women should also have a choice if they don't want to have a natural birth or want to reduce pain. All options should be available."

Dutch mom

Dutch mom

"I think the Dutch midwife system allows for things to be less 'planned'—which is a good thing. It allows the option for (natural) births at home."

"I think midwives in Holland treat birth more as a natural process than as a medical process. This is also because midwives handle birth if there are no complications, whereas doctors are called in when, in fact, there are complications."

Dutch mom

Dutch mom

"Only when I am really ill would I go to a doctor. Giving birth is not an illness. I would prefer an expert (the midwife) at my side who is skilled to guide me through giving birth."

"I would prefer a combination of both: the warmth of the midwife and the medical expertise of a gynaecologist. This gives me assurance."

Dutch mom

Dutch mom

"I prefer a midwife because they have more respect for mother and child. But it is very important that doctors are available when there are complications. Most births don't need a doctor."

Of course, the cost disparity between the two nations begs the question: Is there a correlation between the quality (i.e. safety) and cost of birthing? Unfortunately, despite being the costliest country in the world to give birth in, the United States also has one of the highest rates of both infant and maternal death among industrialised nations.

Average Amount Paid for Childbirth (2012)

	CONVENTIONAL DELIVERY	CAESAREAN
United States	**$9,775**	**$15,041**
Switzerland	4,039	5,186
France	3,541	6,441
Chile	2,992	3,378
Netherlands	2,669	5,328
Britain	2,641	4,435
South Africa	2,035	3,449

Note : Amounts paid are the actual payments agreed to by insurance companies or other payers for services, and are lower than billed charges. Amounts shown include routine prenatal, delivery and postpartum obstetric care. Some care provided by practitioners other than the obstetrician—like ultrasounds performed by a radiologist or blood testing by a lab—are not included in this tally.
Source : International Federation of Health Plans

Midwives

The Dutch maternity system is truly unique as it centres primarily around midwife care. Care is split into two main categories: primary and secondary. Primary care is considered "non-medical" and is specifically for low-risk cases. Primary care is overseen by midwives, and the very occasional general practitioner (GP). GPs, in fact, are only responsible for around 0.5% of all births (and this is mainly in rural areas). Secondary care consists of specialised hospital midwives and obstetricians/gynecologists.

The majority of births in the Netherlands fall under primary care and, thus, are looked after by a midwife. The basic belief behind the entire maternity system is "that a healthy woman with a healthy (low-risk) pregnancy is best taken care of by a midwife. This minimises her chances of receiving unnecessary interventions of any kind, gives her a high standard of care and is furthermore very cost effective" (KNOV, Royal Dutch Organisation of Midwives).

In the Netherlands, there are close to 3,000 active midwives, with 29% of midwives working in a hospital setting. To put the total number of midwives into perspective, there are only 775 active obstetricians/gynecologists working within the entire country.

"Overwhelming evidence points towards a continuity of care model and the empowering effect of a midwife for women, both physically and psychologically."
The Royal Dutch Organisation of Midwives Association (KNOV)

No Worries

Dutch women are relatively relaxed when it comes to their pregnancies. There is no huge panic about what you can or cannot do, and conversations with pregnant Dutch friends or colleagues rarely focus on the laundry list of foods you dare not eat while pregnant. Not surprisingly, the Dutch no-nonsense approach reigns with both moderation and sensibility as recurrent themes in Dutch prenatal care.

Don't get me wrong—you won't find Dutch mothers feasting casually on *filet american* (a uniquely Dutch sandwich spread consisting of raw ground beef) and pounding back a Heineken during their nine months of gestation. However, Dutch mothers-to-be and their associated medical providers keep the risks within perspective.

"Ancient Roman relief carving of a midwife"

I was more than surprised, on my first visit to my Dutch midwife, to notice a gleaming state-of-the-art coffee machine in the waiting room. The fluorescent lights blinked the options of regular, latte, espresso, and so on. "Can I drink coffee?" I asked, utterly surprised. My guide to pregnancy doom and gloom (a.k.a. *What to Expect When You're Expecting*) had strictly forbidden it. My midwife looked amused. "Of course; actually, a recent study found that you can safely have up to five cups a day … but it's always best to trust your own body." I was flabbergasted! "Five cups?! I wouldn't drink that even if I wasn't pregnant!" I replied. Her Dutch reaction was priceless: "Like I said, you know your body best. I'm not your mother." You know your body best—this statement exemplifies the simple, yet powerful, theme underlying Dutch maternity care.

Can I drink it?

During a break at a work conference in Amsterdam—now clearly pregnant—I decided to grab a cup of coffee. An American man looked at me, and then at my coffee, and loudly stated, "Already putting yourself first?" followed by a booming laugh. He followed up with a nervous laugh, "Decaf though, right? Right??"
"Um … no," I replied. "It's actually the real deal."
The complete stranger then went on to say, "Oh well, to heck with the doctor's recommendations. My wife coulda used some coffee these last nine months! You're certainly living on the edge!"
"Well," I stated calmly (as calmly as I could without my morning cuppa), "My Dutch doctor says you can safely have up to five cups a day."
Complete stranger, needing to get the last word in, looks flabbergasted as he says, "Figures! Europeans are nuts! But good luck to you!"

Can I eat it?

While pregnant, I was surprised to see how pervasive North American websites, guides, and apps (such as "Can I Eat It?") had become. When had pregnancy become so complicated that you needed to carry around a smartphone app for 24-7 access to critical diet instructions? What had changed so much across the Atlantic, since the time of our grandmothers, or even our mothers, that merited this new obsessive fear?

*Based on research from ACOG (American Congress of Obstetricians and Gynecologists), the FDA (the U.S. Food & Drug Administration), the ADA (American Dietetic Association) and others, Parenting. com's **Can I Eat It?** offers insight into more than 300 types of meat, poultry, fish, dairy products (mmmm ... cheese), produce, beverages, condiments, and sauces. From anchovies to zucchini, Parenting.com's **Can I Eat It?** has an answer for all of your pregnancy food safety questions.*

Only once did I find myself tempted to download one of the U.S.'s #1 pregnancy apps—"Can I Eat It?". I was having lunch in Amsterdam with a friend from New York and I casually mentioned how I had been craving the strangest things during my pregnancy, namely tabasco sauce and salami. She nearly choked on her *broodje* and immediately freaked out. "Colleen, you're not ALLOWED to eat salami!"

She then proceeded to launch into an extremely loud monologue on the numerous ways something as innocent as salami could endanger my unborn baby. The fear in her voice was palpable and it made me immediately feel sick recalling the many salami sandwiches I had eaten that past week. I jumped on my phone and started Googling; sure enough, babycenter.com had an equally frightening opinion of my lunch choices, and a whole host of other dangerous items I had never heard of at any of my prenatal appointments.

After lunch ended, I dialled my midwife, explaining nervously how I had made a *big* mistake. Luckily, I found that familiar, reassuring Dutch common sense on the other end of the line. My midwife explained that my recent salami indulgences were fine—and so were, in fact, smoked or uncooked ham or dried beef—but everything in moderation, of course. She calmly noted that raw cheese and alcohol were non-negotiables, and for me to remember that, above all, "a calm pregnancy made for a calm baby."

Do pregnant Dutch moms worry less?

"I ate sushi nearly every day of my pregnancy. I knew it was fresh, plus delicious and healthy for me and the baby. The risk is negligible and I was willing to take that risk."

Dutch mom

Dutch mom

"My advice for anyone craving sushi while pregnant: go to the best restaurant in town and ENJOY!"

"I ate raw fish and Parma ham a lot during my pregnancy. My midwife said both were safe as long as the fish was fresh. I trust her and I didn't worry one bit."

Dutch mom

Gezellig ambiance

As I rode my bike down the quiet canal, I looked around and found myself admiring the absolute beauty of this town. The canal houses stood tall, their 16th-century grandeur reflecting off of the still waters. The fact that I could hop on my bike and cruise over to my midwife's office seemed like an utter luxury: no snow to shovel off a frozen car, no traffic jams to endure, no dodgy parking lots to pay for.

As I journeyed along the canals, a metal stork affixed to a canal house letterbox caught my eye—*this must be the place.* I pushed the large wooden door open and stepped into the first floor of the building. I followed a small tiled hallway to a small empty room; sleek Scandinavian-designed furniture greeted me, clean wooden floors, and pastel-painted walls. A small wooden toy kitchen sat in the corner of the room next to a gleaming espresso machine.

As I sat down on one of the wooden chairs, I wondered if I was indeed in the right place. Wasn't there a receptionist or someone I needed to check in with? This was unlike any medical office I had ever been to before.

I thought back to my GP's office in Canada, in which I could very well be sitting now had circumstances been different. The contrast was stark: the Canadian waiting room's metal chairs lined up against the wall of a sterile office full of coughing children, crying babies, and frustrated faces. Wait times were long and patience was short. Two pleasant, but clearly over-worked, receptionists dressed in blue medical smocks sat behind a waist-high counter. Phones incessantly rang, keyboards clacked, and colour-coded medical charts overflowed from the shelves behind them. Paper signs pinned to the walls barked out angry commands: *"Late cancellations WILL be charged,"* *"Prescriptions are NEVER given over the phone!"* and *"A limit of two issues ONLY per appointment."* This passive-aggressive tone hung in the air, adding to an already tense atmosphere.

Here in this peaceful, pleasant house overlooking a canal, things could not have been more different. Back home, big-bellied pregnant women sat amongst the elderly and the ill. Here in Amsterdam, I sat peacefully alone, hearing only the hushed sounds of classical music and murmured chatter coming from the closed room next to me.

Dutch women, whether they know it or not, are afforded the luxury of relaxing and calm environments during their maternity care and birthing experience. Simply not having to sit in an overcrowded doctor's office full of the flu is a massive privilege compared to the rest of the world. Calm, welcoming, and well-decorated offices set the tone for relaxed appointments.

It, however, should not come as too much of a surprise, as the Dutch do have a penchant for the *gezellig* (roughly translatable to cosy, comfortable, a nice atmosphere, a good ambiance, etc.). With a nation somewhat obsessed with all things *gezellig*, it isn't so unusual that this obsession would seep into all aspects of Dutch life, including the birthing process!

Case in point, a quote from the national guide on pregnancy *(GroeiGids)* given to all pregnant women in the Netherlands:

*"**Create your own ambiance:** At a home birth you can create a calming atmosphere by ensuring that there is warm lighting, pleasant music, and generally a comfortable environment in which to give birth. If you are giving birth in hospital, more and more have single-room delivery suites. Every effort will be made to create a comfortable and familiar environment (**read: gezellig!**) For example, you can ask whether there is a CD player or bring your own music player. You can easily create your own ambiance in the maternity unit if you bring a curtain or grand foulard. You could also bring pictures or posters."*

Personalized care

During my pregnancy, my best friend, Karla, came to visit from Canada. I just happened to have a midwife appointment on one of the mornings she was in town. Being a Canadian (OB-GYN) Obstetrician/Gynaecologist, Karla had been carefully following my care and was eager to attend the appointment and get a first-hand glance at the Dutch birth system in action.

Arriving in the empty waiting room office, she too had the same impression as I had had at the appointment along the canal months earlier. *"Where were all the people? Were we at the right place?!"* Once the appointment was in full swing, I saw her scanning the room, the equipment, and taking in everything the midwife was saying. I had come with a list of questions and after the regular checkup, there was time to sit and discuss any questions or concerns I had at this point.

Once the appointment had ended, Karla and I walked down the street to grab a coffee. Taking our places at the local Dutch "brown bar," I was eager to hear what she thought of the appointment and of my midwife. Her first words explained the shocked look on her face: "How long were we in there for? Was that the *normal length* of your appointments?!" I hadn't thought about it at the time, as I never once felt rushed by the midwives. I replied that I guessed we had been there for around 20 minutes and asked how long a typical appointment would be in Canada. "That's amazing! Our doctors would love to have that time," said Karla, "but unfortunately, we probably have five to ten minutes at most!"

The Dutch midwife system allows for a great deal of personalized care. Appointments are lengthy, frequent, and allow for plenty of time to discuss questions and concerns. The midwife practice I attended for both pregnancies had this to say on their homepage:

> ### *We believe in personal care.*
>
> *High-quality personal care means that we guide and support you in a good and safe way. It also means that we help you to understand what is happening during your pregnancy, so that you can make the best choices and can really enjoy this special period. That is why, for example, we take plenty of time during your appointment to explain exactly how your baby is developing, what you can expect during pregnancy and the delivery, and of course to answer all your questions as clearly as we can.*

> *Personal care also means that we tailor our care to your requirements. We listen carefully to what your ideal birth is like and make a birthing plan together with you. We discuss where you can give birth, what kind of painkillers are available and in which positions you can give birth. During the delivery we will give you room to determine what makes you feel good.*

And luckily it wasn't "marketing speak," as my Dutch midwives definitely practiced what they preached!

"My midwife really did her best to empower me, helping me to get rid of my fears and give me the feeling that I could actually do this."

Dutch mom

Dutch mom

"Midwives are less clinical and try to make the whole process a more personal experience."

"One of the best things about the Dutch system is the convenience and personal care. Having check-ups with your local midwife around the corner is really nice, and midwives have a much more personal touch."

Dutch mom

Round-the-clock attention

The Dutch midwife system offers a level of round-the-clock care that, I dare say, cannot be found in other countries. Midwives are reachable 24 hours a day, should you need them. Of course, this does not mean they are available at your every beck and call, but if needed, you know where you can turn at all times.

I was amazed on one of my first visits when my midwife gave me a card with her mobile (cell phone) number. She explained that it was for emergencies outside of office hours, but that if something was truly bothering me or "keeping me up at night" I should not hesitate to call at any time during the night. I was speechless. What an incredible level of service—having the card, and knowing there was someone I could call at any time, was reassuring in itself. I could not imagine the same scenario in Canada, or the United States, where I'd be able to call my own birth practitioner day or night.

> **"If you are worried:** *Call any time you are worried about something. In the evening and at night worries tend to increase. Often a phone call is enough to stem these worries" (Quote from pamphlet given by midwife practice).*

Staying fit and active

During my first trimester, my midwife gave me a handy check-list of "what to do when" during pregnancy. The list covered such necessities as appointments, tests, and ultrasounds, but it also included a curious deadline for joining a "pregnancy gym or prenatal yoga class"—to be started by 24 weeks.

Yoga

At nearly every appointment, I had been asked if I was already enrolled or was planning to follow a yoga class. I found this fascinating, as it wasn't simply a suggestion or an option for "alternative" care, but more so a *firm* recommendation (which actually sounded pretty close to an order).

Prenatal yoga is very common in the Netherlands and highly recommended, as is keeping up regular physical activity.

The class I took combined surprisingly athletic yoga with confidence-building exercises for birthing. It truly did convince me of my body's ability to naturally birth and gave me the confidence to decide, on my own terms, how and where I wanted to birth.

My yoga class may have been a little more "out there" than the norm, but what is true is that Dutch women are encouraged to stay active and fit throughout their pregnancies—and the recommendation to attend a class, go to the gym, or simply to stay active is followed by the vast majority of Dutch women!

"The classes explore the advantages of an active birth, therapeutic stretching-yoga exercises and the practice of all the upright birth positions, which eases the birth process. The emphasis is on a natural safe birth, but also on how to cope with difficulties, methods of intervention and birth at home or in hospital, and ways in which water can be used during pregnancy, labour, and birth. A revolutionary practice to bring the individual in touch with his or her own powers, to have faith in the truth that is found within and confidence in the body's own natural strength" (Quote from the website of the yoga studio I attended in Amsterdam).

LIST: What to arrange:

After 6 weeks of pregnancy

- Register at our practice. Around eight weeks you will have your first appointment at our practice.

Before 11 weeks

- Decide whether you want to have a combination test.
- If you do, make an appointment at the Ultrasound Center.

Between 12 and 16 weeks

- Do you want care for your child after the birth? If so, visit some day-care centres and register your child in one.

- Inform your family doctor and your pharmacist that you are pregnant. This will prevent being prescribed the wrong medication (in an emergency situation), which could be dangerous for the baby.

Between 12 and 18 weeks

- Register at a maternity nurse agency (*kraamzorg*).
- Decide whether you want to have a 20-week ultrasound scan (the anomaly scan). If you do, make an appointment at the Ultrasound Center.

Around 24 weeks

- Join a pregnancy gym or yoga class.
- Parents of a newborn child must observe a number of rules in the Netherlands. Read more about the Family law, before the birth.
- Order (if you want to) things for the baby's room and a pram in good time. An order can take up to ten weeks!

After 33 weeks

- Think about birth announcement cards.
- Visit our free seminar on delivery

At 37 weeks

- Order blocks via *Thuiszorg* (Home Care) to raise the bed. At the time of birth the blocks should be in place under the bed. Also if you are going to give birth in a hospital.

- Have you received the maternity package? You will often receive this automatically via your insurance. Otherwise you can buy it at a drugstore, pharmacy, or home care shop.

After the birth of your baby

- Have someone who was present at the confinement register the birth of the baby at the town hall within three days after the birth of the baby.
- Register the birth of the baby within a week at the insurance company.

"You can simply keep doing what you always did: work, sports, sex, driving, etc. Your body will let you know when it becomes too much. After all, you are not ill, you are pregnant" (Quote from "Pregnancy: Growth Guide" (Groei Gids) given to all expectant women in the Netherlands).

How do pregnant Dutch women stay fit?

"I took prenatal yoga while pregnant. I wouldn't consider that being really physically active, though. But it is very helpful to teach you how to relax and deal with pain."

Dutch mom

Dutch mom

"I stayed active while pregnant and also did prenatal yoga. Yoga helps you breathe and I can say that is pretty important during everyday life, as well as giving birth!"

"It was important for me to stay fit during my pregnancy, as I heard from my midwife this could make the birth easier—and I truly think it did!"

Dutch mom

Dutch mom

"I did birthing classes, but no special sports. I love sports normally, but during my pregnancy I didn't really feel like it, so I just took it easy. Of course, I rode my bike every day, everywhere. But this is not a sport!"

Bumps and bikes

Dutch women see biking as a regular part of daily life and not necessarily a chore or an unusual fitness activity. For this reason, the majority of Dutch women continue to bike throughout their entire pregnancies. I believe that this fact, on its own, keeps Dutch women very fit and healthy during their pregnancies.

Dutch mom

"Did I bike while pregnant? Of course I did, I'm Dutch! I cannot do without my bike. A few days before my son was born in April of 2007 it was really warm for that time of year, so we went for a lovely long bike ride along the Spaarne river. Still have great memories of that tour."

Dutch mom

"I biked until the very end (nine months) and for the first time six days after giving birth (to pick up the birthday cards myself), but I would not recommend that to anyone! Haha!"

"During my first pregnancy I biked until the very last day! Second pregnancy I stopped a lot earlier. Had to do with winter and slippery roads . . ."

Dutch mom

"I biked during my last pregnancy with my one-year-old on the back of the bike. I did this till about seven months, then the bump became too uncomfortable on the bike and I didn't trust my balance getting on and off anymore."

Dutch mom

"I think I probably stopped biking around the eight month (of pregnancy). But also because it was winter time and that is more risky."

Dutch mom

CHAPTER 2

BIRTH

O ver ten years ago in a smoky Dutch brown café, I looked across a plate of *bitterballen* and told my then-boyfriend, "Yes, I could live in Amsterdam … but I could never EVER give birth in this country!" I just couldn't get my head around the Dutch "you must birth at home in your bathtub while burning sage" attitude. My first Dutch doctor was obsessed with the notion of "birth *gezelligheid*." During one of my appointments, she told me about her upcoming labour and how she planned to give birth at home by candlelight, accompanied by her favourite classical music.

My early-twenties-slightly-judgmental-North-American-self could only muster the thought, "OMG, is she part of some Dutch hippy commune?? Time for a new doctor!"

After moving neighbourhoods (and doctors) I realized that she was not part of a commune but simply shared the average Dutch opinion that birth was "not a medical condition" and, as such, did not require extraneous medical interventions. Flash forward 12 years and I have twice given birth naturally in Amsterdam à la Dutch, accompanied by a fabulous doula, super competent midwives, and a supportive hubby! Lesson learned: Never say never!

The Dutch are pioneers of the modern-day home birth. Although numbers have decreased over time, and sadly continue to. In 2014, 13% of all births in the Netherlands took place at home—with another sizable percentage of women attempting to do so. Compare this to the less than two percent of births taking place in homes in France, Belgium, Germany, and the U.K. each year, and you can see how the Dutch have been—and remain today—the leaders in homebirths in the Western world.

Of course, giving birth in the comfort of one's home also implies doing so without body-numbing and mind-altering substances. Is that a gasp I hear? Yes, Dutch women are a tough breed and notorious for their drug-free births. Even in hospitals, only six percent of Dutch women have an epidural. Across the Atlantic, things are precisely the opposite. A recent study shows that only six percent of women in large American hospitals opted for a drug-free birth.

Are Dutch women genetically superior? Do they not feel pain like the rest of the world? Or are they seriously just tougher? Had all that *filet americain* and *drop* gone to their heads? I believe that the truth is actually rather simple and boils down to three important factors:

- ✔ Dutch women are better prepared for the realities of birth.

- ✔ Dutch women have significantly less fear of the pain involved in labour.

- ✔ Dutch women accept pain as a natural and necessary part of the experience.

Let's examine these factors and see what Dutch moms "like" about birth in the Netherlands!

In this Chapter

Freedom to choose

Freedom of choice plays a central role in the Dutch maternity system. With the Dutch belief that childbirth is natural, many choices are offered to women on the basis of their personal situation (low risk vs. high risk), and their own preferences. The freedom to choose how and where you will give birth is a fundamental right in the Netherlands, empowering Dutch women in the very early stages of their pregnancies. The Royal Dutch Organisation of Midwives Association (KNOV) praises the Netherlands for having a particularly *vrouwvriendelijk geboorte* system (female-friendly birth system).

If you are giving birth in the Netherlands and you are deemed "low risk" you are able to choose the location and type of birth you wish. This means deciding whether you feel more comfortable in your own home, at the hospital (with your midwife), at the hospital with a doctor, or in a birthing centre, or "birth hotel." Water births are also possible at home, in birth centres, and are now even available in many hospitals. Even for medicalized births, many options are still possible for the labouring women. Many hospitals for example have wireless monitoring so that women can move around freely (even in the birth pool). Birthing balls are freely available so expecting mothers can stay upright during labour and birth stools can be used to give birth in an upright position.

Birth support

Doulas are becoming more popular in the Netherlands. A doula's role is to provide support during pregnancy, birth, and the postnatal period. A doula tailors their services to the needs of their client; provides informational support while pregnant; provides emotional support before, during, or after the birth;

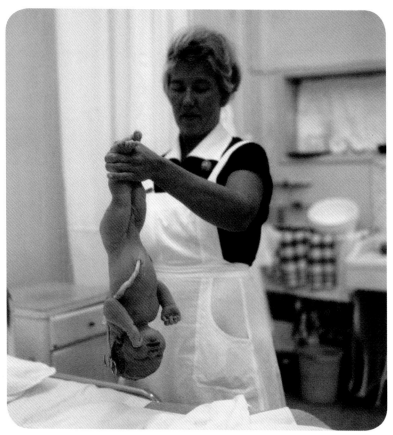

Dutch nurse/midwife 1965–75

"Births with a doula usually are shorter and are often less painful and associated with significantly fewer complications" (Quote on the popular Dutch parenting website Oei, ik groei!)

"Pregnant women consider freedom of choice to be essential. The midwife provides objective and clear information about the benefits and disadvantages of different choices in each phase of care. Based on this information and her own expectations, the pregnant woman can make a well-informed decision. This also applies to the decision of where to give birth: at home, in a birthing centre or in an outpatient clinic in a hospital. Healthy women can choose to give birth at home. The choice for home birth is a responsible one; it is safe and has a favourable effect on the course of childbirth" (The Royal Dutch Organisation of Midwives Association [KNOV])

and provides active physical support during labour; or a combination of all of the above. Although the concept of a doula is better known in North America, I found my midwives—and even my gynaecologist—completely open to the idea, in the Dutch spirit of "freedom to choose!".

The presence of a doula is said to lower the risk of unnecessary interventions and possible complications. A study published in 2014 in the American Journal of Managed Care found that births with a doula had "an almost 60 percent reduction in women's odds of having a C-section, and 80 percent lower odds of having a non-medically indicated C-section compared with women who had no doula."

"Childbirth is a physical, emotional and spiritual experience, with long-term impact on a woman's personal well-being. As a certified doula I will support you and your partner using encouragement, water, acupressure, massage, positioning and other tools as needed. Labour is a dance between a woman and her baby; my role is defined by your needs. My goal is to support parents in having a positive and memorable birth experience and a gentle beginning for their baby" (Quote from the website of my Doula, Jennifer Walker).

While pregnant with my first child, I opted to hire a doula to support me during the process. I felt I wanted someone who knew how to navigate the Dutch medical system, should I need it. Although I had been reassured by the quality of the care I was receiving, I felt a doula could further prepare and support me and my husband in case I had to be transferred to a hospital.

This actually turned out to be the case, as during labour I was abruptly transferred to a hospital with a doctor and nurses I had never met before. So I was relieved and grateful to have a familiar and highly experienced birth companion at my side. During my hospital birth, the three of us—myself, my husband, and my doula—were alone together 90% of my labour and formed the perfect trio of empowered love, comfort, and support.

What do moms living in the Netherlands think of the Dutch birth system?

"I am 30 weeks pregnant and I am able to make all the decisions I want. For instance: I would like to give birth in a birth centre and if the pain is too much, they will transport me to the hospital next door for pain medication, etc. If the first birth goes well, I definitely would like to try to give birth at home the second time."

Dutch mom-to-be

"I think the Dutch are leading the way in home births/ natural births because it's proven to be better and safer for mother and child, recommended by World Health Organization and other health organizations. But you can always choose to have your baby at a birthing centre or a hospital (the insurance does pay but you pay a little bit too—eigen bijdrage). And if you ask, a doctor will always give you pain relief medication (except if you're at the 'pushing' phase; then they can't give it to you)."

Brazilian mom (living in NL)

"The most important thing is that a mother feels empowered, whatever decision she makes with regards to her pregnancy and birth. Whether this is at home, in hospital, with drugs, without drugs, with a midwife or with a doctor—the woman should be central in all decisions. The Dutch system allows for this."

Dutch mom

"In the Netherlands you have a lot of free choice about how and where you want to birth."

Dutch mom

"The biggest strength of the Dutch system is that you have CHOICE. I would say that is the most important aspect of giving birth; giving the child in your womb the chance to decide for itself when he/she/they want to be born."

Dutch mom

Home birth

Low-risk women may choose whether to give birth at home or in a hospital (outpatient clinic). This free choice for the place of birth is almost unique in the Western world and is an important pillar of the Dutch maternity system.

In 2014, 13.4% of all Dutch births took place at home. This is a significantly lower figure from years gone by, as during the 1970s the home birth rate was as high as 70%. The '70s and '80s saw a sharp decline to around 35%. This figure remained fairly constant until 2004 when the first Peristat report was released. At the same time, a recent research revealed that 82% of women want to keep the possibility for the choice of home births (KNOV).

> *"The number of women giving birth with a community midwife is decreasing while overwhelming evidence points towards a continuity of care model and the empowering effect of a midwife for women, both physically and psychologically"***(The Royal Dutch Organisation of Midwives Association [KNOV]).**

Low-risk home births are safer than hospital

The conclusions of a large-scale study conducted in the Netherlands were released in the summer of 2013. The results shocked many, as data collected from some 147,000 low-risk women in primary (midwife) care showed overwhelming evidence that births were safer at home for the mother than in hospital.

> *"Results: Overall, 92,333 (62.9%) women had a planned home birth and 54,419 (37.1%) a planned hospital birth.*
>
> *Conclusions: Low-risk women in primary care at the onset of labour with planned home birth had lower rates of severe acute maternal morbidity, postpartum haemorrhage, and manual removal of placenta than those with planned hospital birth.*

For parous women these differences were statistically significant. Absolute risks were small in both groups. There was no evidence that planned home birth among low-risk women leads to an increased risk of severe adverse maternal outcomes in a maternity care system with well trained midwives and a good referral and transportation system" (British Medical Journal: BMJ 2013;346:f3263).

"Planned home births are less risky than planned hospital births, particularly for second-time mothers, says research in the British Medical Journal. A large Dutch study found the risk of severe complications to be one in 1,000 for home births and 2.3 in 1,000 for hospital births" (BBC News: Home birth complications 'less common' than hospital).

"This comes from a good risk selection system, good transport in place and well-trained midwives. Women who give birth at home are less likely to have interventions at home, but if there is a serious problem there should be a good system to deal with them" (Ank de Jonge, a practicing midwife and senior researcher on the study from the VU University Medical Centre in Amsterdam).

What are your thoughts on home births?

"I had my second baby at home. No candles, no music, no 'plan' because what are you planning? It can take two hours or 48, come on . . . Just giving birth in your own bed is really nice and private. Just me, my hubby, the midwife and the nurse, small and intimate. To say I loved it . . . it's still giving birth, which is always an amazing experience, but I wouldn't call it fun. But the privacy, your own home, bathroom and fridge, all the attention is for your new baby and I thought it was pretty damn sweet! AND the nurse stays there for ten days, to check on you and your baby, do the chores, and make coffee with beschuit met muisjes *for your family and friends! Don't put it down until you've lived it!"*

Dutch mom

"I just had my second baby here in the Netherlands, both in hospital. I would have liked to try it at home if I had been allowed (medical conditions meant hospital for me). As an American I first thought birth without drugs would be a crazy thing, but in the end I wished for a drug-free experience."and I truly think it did!"

American mom (living in NL)

"I think everyone should be able to choose whatever they want for their own birth. You can do that here."

Dutch mom

"I was convinced home births were a CRAZY idea and utter nonsense. Once I saw the facts about their outcomes and safety, I was tempted to have my first at home. But I suppose in the end, I still couldn't get my head completely around my Canadian misconceptions, so I opted for a hospital birth—with a midwife."

Canadian mom

"As a Dutch husband, I saw four of our five children entering the world AT HOME! The fifth too, we did it together, because the GP was too late! My wife was a turbo-birthing mother! I pulled out our daughter very gently and laid her on my wife. I asked the doctor, when she ran up the stairs, 'Well, can I get the 50% of your wage? I did the job!'"

Dutch dad

"Never say never! I swore I wanted a hospital birth, with a doctor, drugs (epidural) and all, but my labour went very quickly and in that moment I decided to stay at home. I felt safe. I felt in good care and I realized at home was the best place for me! Of course, my friends and family back home were SHOCKED and could not believe it, but it was one of the best decisions I ever made!"

American mom (living in NL)

Dutch mom-to-be

"As a Dutchie, I can never wrap my head around my Dutch friends' insistence to deliver at home, au natural. Why put yourself through it? It's like breaking your arm and saying, 'Oh, I don't need a cast, that's unnatural: I'll just let it flap around on its own till it's fine,' or 'No, no, dentist, you can pull out two of my wisdom teeth au natural, the pain is part of life.' Are these people crazy? Of course, to each their own, everyone decides for themselves."

"To us, it has always been normal to have home deliveries. And no, these aren't all with candles and bath tubs, usually they are just in the comfort of your own bed, in your own home, which makes you feel more relaxed than being in some sterile, impersonal room in a hospital. And home deliveries are just as safe as hospital ones, and when a doctor has an inkling you might get complications, you will be referred to the hospital ahead of the delivery anyway."

Dutch mom

Dutch mom (in Canada)

"Being Dutch and telling about the birth of my son to my Canadian friends (at home, no painkillers), I was their hero of the day."

"Some people tend to not realise that giving birth is a medical activity, not just a personal experience. So you might plan your perfect delivery with candles, music etc., but in the end, two lives are involved."

Dutch mom

"I was so scared of giving birth, but my midwives were incredible. I had planned on going to the hospital, but when the time came, together with my midwife and husband we decided to stay home. The labour was fast and furious, and it was incredibly special to welcome my new baby girl into the world in our own home (and bed!) surrounded by love and support."

British mom (living in NL)

"Sorry to say I'm not a fan of home births. If something goes wrong, a hospital is safer."

Dutch mom

"I'm not too sure about home birthing anymore. Due to circumstances, I had to give birth in the hospital both times. In the end I was glad I did; I had no stress of having to move during labour like some of my friends had. You now see more and more geboorte hotels attached to a hospital coming up. I think that is the ideal solution: homey environment, but everything at hand if needed."

Dutch mom

"Dutch doctors don't make you DO stuff, they give you advice. If you want to go to the hospital, fine, do so. If your pregnancy isn't totally standard, they'll send you to the hospital and the rest of your pregnancy, and the delivery, will be dealt with by a gynaecologist team. If YOU want to go to the hospital, you do so. If YOU want drugs, you get them."

Dutch mom

Prepare for the unexpected

Around my 28th week of pregnancy, an enormous box showed up on my doorstep. I managed to haul it inside and was itching to see what the crate-sized package contained. A baby gift from Canada, perhaps? Exciting! I ripped open the box and rifled through the contents, only to first pull out a package of latex rubber gloves. Huh? This was followed by a large bottle of rubbing alcohol. Confused, I checked the address on the package once again. No mix-up here, it was clearly addressed to me.

What a curious collection of items! My midwife had mentioned a delivery of "baby items" from my health insurance company, but I had imagined something entirely different: bottles, nappies, diaper cream perhaps, but certainly not the likes of an enormous first-aid box!

The contents jolted me out of the zen-like birth scenario I had imagined. Why on earth were so many rubber sheets needed? Those baby diapers were not diapers at all, but some sort of elephant-esque female sanitary pads! Dozens of rubber gloves, two umbilical cord clips, and endless spools of sterile cotton lay before me. It looked more like the medical supplies needed for a team trek up the Himalayas. Good gosh, I thought, it looked like things were about to get very real!

Dutch mothers are provided, in most cases by their insurance providers, a set of items to prepare for the birth and after-period. This is referred to as the *kraampakket*.

The standard package normally includes:

- a rubber mattress protection sheet
- mattress mats and pads
- post-birth sanitary napkins
- disposal stretch panties
- cotton pads/wadding
- sterile gauze pads
- digital thermometer
- rubbing alcohol
- disinfectant soap
- umbilical cord clamps

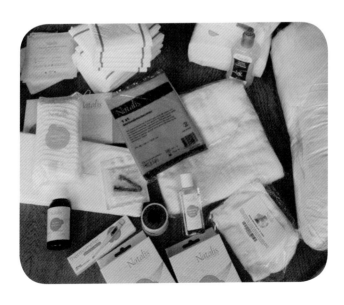

The Dutch "maternity package" is not part of the basic health insurance policy, but is included with the majority of supplementary packages. In the case where insurance does not cover the package, they can be bought online or at most drugstores for an affordable 25–50 euros (and these costs can often also be claimed back from insurance). The concept is rather basic; however, it ensures that all Dutch moms get off to a good (and safe!) start with the necessary items in their home.

Thoughts on the Dutch "maternity package" (*kraampakket*)

"I know it's super handy, but that package scared me when it arrived!"

Dutch mom

If this package arrived on my doorstep when I was pregnant, I would run for the hills! Just sayin'..."

Canadian mom

"The kraampakket is impressive! But giving birth is messy so you need it! A lot of it is also very useful when you come back from the hospital too, so not just for home births as some people think."

Dutch mom

Dutch mom

"These are the kinds of things you just assume are standard practice in all countries. But I know it is a luxury [in the Netherlands] to have the choice of home births, and the most helpful care after birth of a kraamzorgster."

Pain is normal—have no fear!

During my pregnancy, my midwife gave me a Dutch pamphlet which was handed out to all expecting mothers in the Netherlands. Scanning the first paragraph, the Dutch direct tone was quite clear: "Giving birth hurts. There is no way to ignore this. But every birth is different. How much pain you will have and where exactly, no one can predict." A similar message was repeated on the midwife practice's website:

> "Giving birth is painful. No one can avoid this. Every woman experiences pain in a different way and some can cope better with pain than others. Now that you are pregnant you might well be wondering about pain during delivery. How bad will it be? But don't worry too much about this: there is a variety of ways to soften the pain, with and without medication, at home and in a hospital" **(The Royal Dutch Organisation of Midwives Association [KNOV]).**

There is no denying that the Dutch like to keep things real. You can observe this pragmatic and practical approach in practically all day-to-day dealings with the Dutch; therefore, it should come as no surprise that these traits are also omnipresent in the Dutch realms of birth.

Dutch society has managed to maintain the ever-important knowledge that childbirth is, in fact, the most natural part of our existence and something not to be feared or unnecessarily interfered with.

Who's afraid of a little pain? Not the Dutch!

"As a Dutch woman, I felt the need to give birth without drugs here in the U.S. There was no question about it for me! I almost felt I needed to do this to honour my Dutch mom and grandmothers. And honestly, why suffer through so much pain? Too much pride, I guess…"

Dutch mom (in the U.S.)

"My wife delivered at home in our own bed. All natural, no drugs, no sterile surroundings. Now I'm not going to voice an opinion on what is best (home/hospital) since I'm not the one who had to go through the pain, but what she said afterwards was something like: 'The beauty of birth outweighs the pain. Delivering at home adds greatly to this beauty so getting drugged is for (and I quote) zeikwijven.' All I can say is I never respected my wife as much as during that period."

Dutch dad

"I gave birth to my daughter while in Australia and was so happy to know that IF I wanted drugs during the delivery IN the hospital, I would get them. Why be in pain? Strangely enough though, my Dutch genes kicked in during the delivery and the knowledge that I could get drugs any time I wanted was enough for me to bear the pain. Until her head came out, when I could no longer control myself and screamed, 'Give me an epidural or any other shit and do it NOW' (in that I-Am-In-Giving-Birth-Pain-Screeching-Voice-From-Hell). It was too late to administer anything and I gave birth to my baby drug-free (unwillingly, haha). Nevertheless, I am very glad I did not give birth at home in the Netherlands."

Dutch mom (living in AUS)

American mom

"*You get pain relief for everything else, why not childbirth? You Dutch people are medieval. And as for complications, things can go wrong in minutes, so you better hope you live next door to a hospital.*"

"*I'm such a baby; I don't even like going to the dentist without drugs, let alone give birth.*"

American mom

REPLY: "*I would choose giving birth over a visit to the dentist any day . . . Yes, all natural, being a Dutchie and all.*"

Dutch mom

"*Unfortunately, more and more Dutch women are losing trust in their natural power and go to hospital. It's a pity, but medicalisation in all parts is taking place here, too. It's logical, fear creates pain!*"

Dutch mom

"*It's the fear that hurts most, not the giving birth!*"

Dutch mom

The focus within society and the press on the dangers of childbirth has had an effect on women and healthcare professionals, an indication of this is the rise of hospital births and an increase in requests for epidural anaesthesia. Within this challenging context the KNOV and her members strive towards keeping pregnancy normal and safe by investing in evidence based integrated team work so that all women can receive continuity of care from a midwife plus the additional care of a specialist (obstetrician) when necessary" **(The Royal Dutch Organisation of Midwives Association [KNOV]).**

Drug-free

Giving birth in your own home also means leaving behind the comforts of body-numbing and mind-altering substances. Dutch women are globally notorious for their drug-free births. In 2013 only 18.4% of all births in the Netherlands were with an epidural. This is still a significantly low figure, when compared to that of Canada or the United States (53.7% and 60% respectively). However, the Dutch figure has been steadily on the rise in the past decade with rates as low as 11.3% in 2008 and 6.2% in 2004.

Dutch moms and drugs: it's not what you think!

Dutch mom

"In the Netherlands, they don't treat birth as a medical condition, it is a thing your body should be able to do under normal circumstances!"

"I, as a Dutchie, am baffled by all the options women in the U.S. have. Epidural, laughing gas . . . I suppose to us it seems U.S. women are either very afraid of pain, or are slightly alleen de lusten, niet de lasten. How to translate this . . . 'just the fun, not the pain' doesn't quite cut it, but I think you get my drift."

Dutch mom

Dutch mom

"In America, you go to the hospital and tell the doctors what to do, because you are an MD, fresh out of Google University. I can't believe that, and if you are wrong, you can always sue them blind."

"The point everyone here seems to disregard is the pure fact that giving natural birth gives the mother a very big boost of self-confidence. It's an accomplishment you can really be proud of and nobody can ever take that feeling away from you."

Dutch mom

American mom

"I had one baby with an epidural and HATED it! Had my second drug-free in a hospital and it was the best experience of my life! There is a reason why there are so many C-sections and inductions in the U.S. and it is because we over-medicate what doesn't need to be medicated at all. Drug-free means less interference means less complications. The rest of the world could learn a lot from the way the Dutch do birth!"

"I'd dare say that it's common sense that a drug-free birth is better for the baby. Just like not drinking alcohol and smoking is better for the baby during pregnancy."

Dutch mom

"I will say they did give me drugs when I asked for them here in NL."

American mom (living in NL)

Time to go home!

With the birth of our daughter, I had complications and thus had to stay in hospital an additional night for monitoring. However, with our son's birth, I was home, sitting on the couch, within a matter of hours. I'll never forget after the delivery, asking a nurse whether I would be getting a meal. She looked at me, confused, "Well, lunch isn't served until 12:00, and I don't think you will be here by then."

Sure enough, two hours after delivery, hospital staff started moving in and shuffling things about in my room. Don't get me wrong, it wasn't as if I was being kicked out, per se, but I did get the feeling it was time to go. Perhaps that common saying shouted out from bartenders at closing time, back home in my college days, would apply:

"You don't have to go home, but you can't stay here!"

As one Dutch nurse surmised, "Why would you want to stay here any longer than needed?" The Dutch, you see, believe that the best place for a healthy mom and babe, after birth, is in their own home—away from the germs and infections lurking around hospital corners.

Mothers and their brand-new babies spend, on average, less than 24 hours in a Dutch hospital after birth. In fact, mothers can leave as soon as four hours after the birth if there are no complications. The idea behind this policy is that the safest place for a new baby and recovering woman is in her own home, with the care of a professional maternity nurse (*kraamzorg*). This is to prevent unnecessary infections in both the new baby and mother. Of course, if any medical complications are present, mom and baby will be required to stay longer.

Why do Dutch moms head home so soon after giving birth?

American mom (living in NL)

"I was in and out of the hospital in—literally—a matter of hours. My son's birth was less than an hour, and afterwards I was exhausted and resting, when the nurses and midwives were like, 'Okay! All good, it's time to go!' I was like, 'umm . . . I just birthed a human here, can I maybe get a moment, or lunch or something first?'"

"A Dutch friend of mine delivered in a hospital years ago, but was quick to point out she went home the same day (!) and was sweeping the floor and cleaning the bathroom the same day."

Dutch dad-to-be

"Why would you want to stay any longer in a hospital than you have to? I was happy to leave immediately after all three of my kids births and be in the comfort of my own home/bed."

Dutch mom

Dutch mom

"It has been proven that is much safer to leave the hospital after having a baby. Hospitals are for sick people and are full of diseases and germs. Why stay there?"

"I think we have a very good infrastructure and small country. Maybe it comes from our Calvinistic background? I wonder if it is not also less expensive than staying in a hospital."

Dutch mom

Dutch mom

"I wonder if the system is based on money or economics? Does it make more financial sense, keeping women in hospital? Or perhaps other countries are just clueless about the human ecosystem."

CHAPTER 3

DUTCH BIRTH
TRADITIONS

At one of my first midwife appointments, I noticed an overflowing basket of cards sitting curiously on the floor next to me. I reached over and sifted through the greetings. Bright bold names were written across the folded paper: Sem, Levi, Mila, Thijs, Roos. These unusual names of newly-arrived infant Amsterdammers were completely foreign to me. I rifled through the basket, fascinated by the names (*was Levi for a girl or boy? And how about Roos? How was it correctly pronounced?*), and by the very cards themselves. Each card prominently mentioned the baby's name and birthdate followed by the parents' names, full home address, and phone number. I presumed this was some sort of cultural standard and made a note in my iPhone to "investigate Dutch birth announcements."

After that visit, I quickly realized that giving birth in the Netherlands would bring forth a host of new Dutch traditions currently unknown to myself and my partner. It seemed the *geboortekaart* (birth card) was of some importance in the Netherlands. Heck, it was even mentioned on the "What to arrange" handout from my midwife practice (33 weeks: Think about birth announcement cards). What other cultural oddities surrounding pregnancy and birth would I soon discover?

I set out to find what traditions Dutch moms like, and not surprisingly found quite a few!

In this Chapter

 Growth guides
🍼 Birth cards/announcements
🍼 *Beschuit met muisjes*
🍼 Stork in your garden/window

Growth Guides (de GroeiGids)

Many people would argue that the Dutch Growth Guides are not a tradition, per se, but I would argue to the contrary. They are an institution in themselves, and are omnipresent throughout a Dutch mother's entire child-rearing years. From the very early advice on conception, to topics like sex-education tips for your teenager, the Growth Guides cover it all and more! They form the backbone of all pregnancy, postnatal, and child-related care in the Netherlands.

The Growth Guide series consists of seven practical books, given free to all prospective and current parents in the Netherlands. They are:

- Planning for Parenthood (*Kinderwens*)
- Pregnancy (*Zwanger*)
- Breastfeeding (*Borstvoeding*)
- Postnatal period (*Kraamtijd*)
- 0-4 years old (0-4 *jaar*)
- 4-12 years old (4-12 *jaar*)
- Puberty (*Puberteit*)

The Growth Guide series is owned by the City of Amsterdam and produced in collaboration with the Public Health Department (GGD) of Amsterdam. The editorial content of the books is developed in collaboration with a network of key partners—namely, midwives, doctors, maternity agencies, lactation consultants, and various municipal departments and experts in the field of youth health and development.

"In the Growth Guide you will find a great deal of information concerning pregnancy and the development, health, and parenting of your child in the various phases of life. You will also be able to find practical tips for the sometimes troublesome and difficult moments in parenting.

"The Growth Guide can also serve as a handbook for the many major and minor doubts or concerns which, in practice, all parents are faced with. With the conveniently arranged table of contents, you can easily find the subject you want to know more about."
– *GroeiGids*

Birth cards / announcements

In Canada, new parents usually send out a birth announcement of some sort, but they are most often of the "Anne Geddes" variety (a.k.a. naked-newborns-in-milk-crates) or the "hey friends, check out our happy postpartum family" photo. Interestingly, I learned that here in the Netherlands the *geboortekaart* was the catalyst for a series of important post-birth rituals. Sending out the card was as much a birth announcement as it was a signal of your readiness for visitors and the official invitation of sorts for the *kraamvisite*. It was, in this regard, also a very practical way of informing friends, family, and colleagues of your address and phone numbers that were needed for arranging an upcoming visit.

Although the *kraamvisite* plays a central role in the traditional birth announcement today, I found that the roots of the Dutch birth card dated back to the mid-1800s and were used as a means of informing an entire village of a baby's successful birth—which was not always a given at the time. In the 1800s, the card took the form of a letter and was reserved for only the wealthiest of Dutch who could afford the significant additional expense. The birth letters of the 19th and 20th centuries included the name and sex of the new arrival as well as the names of both parents.

Beschuit met muisjes

Next in the line-up of Dutch birth traditions is the beloved *beschuit met muisjes*, literally translating in English to "rusk mice." If you've ever been lucky enough to celebrate the birth of a baby in the Lowlands, you will have surely experienced this unique culinary treat. It turns out that after Dutch women birth their babies, they immediately head to the kitchen, grab some *beschuiten* (i.e. rusks: a twice baked piece of round toast), slap on a thick layer of butter, and adorn it with sprinkles—either pink and white (for a girl) or blue and white (for a boy).

Muisjes are not your standard form of candy sprinkles, as they are, in fact, sugar-covered anise seeds. The precise reason why these candy-coated seeds got their interesting name (yes, "mice") is still up for debate. Some say they were named after mice due to their association with fertility, whereas others argue it is simple due to their shape (as once the seeds are covered with sugar they appear to have little tails).

FACT: Orange *muisjes* were sold en-masse for one week in December of 2003, to honour the birth of crown princess Amalia.

I learned the hard way that it is of critical importance to never confuse these sprinkles for their sugary cousin, hagelslag. *Having once mistakenly referred to* muisjes *as* hagelslag *on my blog, I was inundated with literally hundreds of comments, tweets, messages, and emails correcting my serious faux pas. The messages ranged from informative (kindly supplying links and supporting sources) to slightly snarky ("How could a blogger who writes about Dutch culture make such a basic mistake?!") to the downright annoyed (and I quote: "This is WRONG.* Muisjes *are NOT* hagelslag, *and* hagelslag *are NOT* muisjes!!!").*

Once, over lunch, my Dutch boss Antoine tried, through embarrassed mumbles, to explain how the tradition came about. Through his muttering, I gathered something about anise seeds shrinking a woman's . . . errhh . . . lady parts. At that point in the conversation, we both decided to rapidly change the subject ("How about this crazy weather, eh?") as his face was turning a shade of red I'd never seen before and his lack of proper female anatomic terms in English was making for a seriously awkward conversation. Back at my desk, a little Googling revealed that anise seeds are thought to be good for stimulating lactation and returning the uterus to its normal size. It turns out Antoine knew what he was talking about! Of course, this still doesn't explain why the Dutch decided to serve beschuit muisjes to all their guests ("Come on, folks: let's all shrink our wombs back to size together!").

Stork decorations

Coming home from work one day, I happened upon yet another Dutch birth tradition. Cycling up to my apartment in Amsterdam, I couldn't help but notice something sticking out of my neighbour's window. I glanced up, first thinking that perhaps a workman was washing the windows—and then noticed an ENORMOUS stork plastered to the window pane. This one was a no-brainer: the round-bellied new neighbour who had just moved in below us must have given birth!

In European folklore, the stork has always been a symbol of good luck, and the legend of storks bringing babies to new parents dates back centuries with versions found across the globe from Germany to remote corners of Scandinavia, over to the Philippines and back across the ocean to North and South America. Many suggest that the "stork story" became popular across so many cultures and countries as it conveniently alleviated the need and discomfort of discussing sex and procreation with children.

The Dutch tradition of placing life-sized storks in windows or gardens is actually said to have "flown" over from Germany. Although a cute idea, we decided to give this one a pass! I wasn't sure I wanted the birth announced for all to see, and adding a stork to our window seemed to be like an open invitation! The impending *kraamvisite* already had me concerned that after giving birth my house would be overrun with guests.

CHAPTER 4

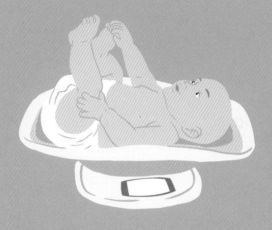

LIFE WITH BABY

Dutch moms are offered extraordinary care during the post-natal period in the Netherlands. The maternity care system of *kraamzorg* is unlike any other country, and arguably superior to all other systems. Mothers are given time to rest, recover, and be supported by trained experts in their own homes. Aside from the *kraamzorg*, the *kraamvisite* is also a very Dutch tradition that further supports mothers in a critical and often isolating time. During the post-natal period, care is transferred from the *kraamzorg* nurse to the Dutch network of *consultatiebureaus*, a "well clinic" for children's health and development. These three pillars of "after-care" lay the foundation for a stable and supportive start to motherhood.

Let's take a closer look at the system of post-natal care in the Netherlands, and how Dutch women are eased into their new roles as mothers with guidance, individual attention, and support.

In this Chapter

- *Kraamzorg*
- *Kraamvisite*
- *Consultatiebureau*

Kraamzorg

She was an utter blessing. She came into our life one sunny morning, bringing sunshine and hope. She was like a breath of fresh air, sent from the heavens above. I suppose I should clear things up right away, before I get too carried away. You see, I'm not talking about our brand-new baby girl (although she was all those things and more), but—in fact—my dear Dutch kraamzorg *nurse!*

The idea of being sent home from the hospital a matter of hours after birthing can be downright scary to most foreigners. In other countries, after giving birth, it is customary to stay in the hospital anywhere from 2-7 days. The idea of being whisked out of the room shortly after delivery makes many a new (foreign) mother's head spin, especially when compared to the standards of their home countries; 1-2 days being the average in Canada and America, 4-5 days in France, and in Japan, a stay of up to a week is not unusual.

The Dutch believe that mother and baby are safer in their own home after giving birth—avoiding any possible complications from hospital-borne infections. The Dutch know, however, that their system can allow for such an early discharge, as essentially you are sent home with an incredible post-baby gift: your very own nurse!

Maternity care in the Netherlands is unlike any other country, and I believe, superior to all other systems. All new moms in the Netherlands are entitled to eight days of care by a highly trained maternity nurse directly after birth. Your midwife will also come by to check up on you and the baby—at least twice during the first week, and possibly more if needed.

The number of maternity care hours you receive is based on the "National Indication Protocol for Maternity Care." The maximum is 80 hours over the course of ten days. The costs of your *kraamzorg* care is reimbursed, for the most part by basic insurance. If you do not have an additional insurance policy, you will pay a very reasonable € 4.15 per hour (2015 rates) for the care.

The purpose of the *kraamzorg* nurse is to help in the postnatal recovery and care of mother and baby. The responsibilities of the nurse include:

- Breastfeeding support and advice
- Care of newborn (checking of all dirty diapers!)
- Daily health checks of mother (temperature, pulse, mental state, stitches, breasts)
- Daily health checks of baby (temperature, state of dirty diapers, weight)
- Meal preparation
- Care of older children
- House cleaning

Kraamzorg nurses have a checklist of itemised duties they must perform each day. The most important of these tasks (i.e. taking the mother and baby's temperature, as well as the baby's weight) is recorded diligently in the "*kraam* diary" along with other observations, such as the mother's physical and mental state. The importance of postnatal care is critical for new mothers, and also in the prevention of postpartum depression and mood disorders. Both my nurses were well-versed in these topics and were able to differentiate between the 'baby blues' and something more serious.

Both of my *kraamzorg* nurses were highly caring, ultra-efficient, and incredible women. They came into our home, giving me both the care and privacy I needed, and immediately started doing laundry, cooking meals, tidying up, and helping with the new baby. I truly couldn't believe the level of kindness and helpfulness. They managed to give us both their company and our privacy when needed. With my firstborn, I had a million-and-one questions: "Was I doing this right?" "Was I supposed to feel this way?" "Was she supposed to cry this much?" and so on. My six-foot, blonde Dutch nurse, Maya (who had three grown daughters of her own) patiently answered each and every one of my questions, in between diligently sterilizing my toilet, bath, and shower, and preparing our snacks and meals. My husband was most impressed when she came to our home each morning, gave the baby a cuddle and asked us how we would like our eggs cooked!

The secrets to how Dutch moms survive the first few weeks

Dutch mom (living in U.K.)

"I am Dutch but all our children were born in the U.K. After our babies were born, I was dismissed out of hospital within two days—with no kraamzorg*!! I felt fortunate that I was able to fly in support, it would otherwise have been a struggle to look after a newborn and toddler(s) so soon after a C-section."*

"I think kraamzorg is a wonderful thing. Really helps you through the first days of being a mom."

Dutch mom

Dutch mom

"Nothing can prepare you for breastfeeding, diaper changing, etc. beforehand, so it is really helpful to have someone in your home to teach you all of this. You do have to hope for someone you click with, though. At one point, I had one that was more of a burden in the end. Didn't bother me that much, but I remember getting a text from my husband that he was hiding out at the neighbours', because he couldn't stand her anymore."

"The best thing ever. I would even apply for the extended version that I have heard other moms talk about."

Dutch mom

Dutch mom

"In my opinion it's the best thing the Netherlands have to offer. Advice and help from a non-family member (who leaves again, and doesn't judge you). Great!"

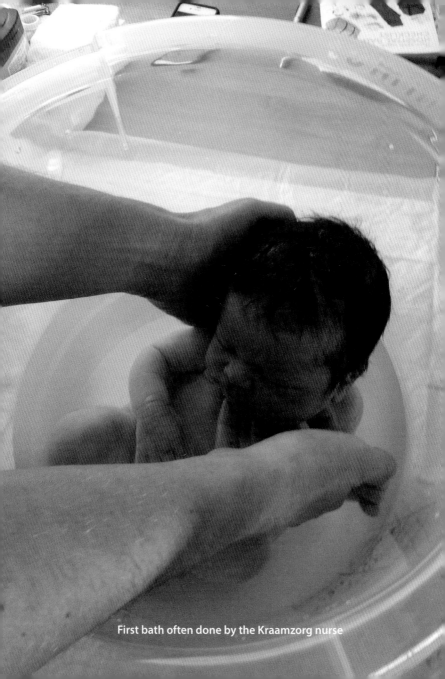

First bath often done by the Kraamzorg nurse

"I am highly in favour of the system. Walking out of a hospital with a newborn is highly confusing and I personally loved having a skilled person by my side for the first few days. It gave me peace of mind taking care of my baby, time to recuperate from a C-section, and an understanding pair of ears for my stories and a practical set of hands. Of course, how it works out is highly dependent on the kraamverpleegster you get, but the lady who came to our house was a member of the family the moment she walked in the door."

Dutch
mom

"It is very nice to be in your own safe environment and get support in your own home."

Dutch
mom

"I think the kraamzorg system originated from a tradition of giving birth at home (and not in the hospital) like is common in other (Western) countries. It is a gift!"

Dutch
mom

Kraamzorg nurse weighing the baby at home in Amsterdam

Rave reviews from international moms

American mom (living in NL)

"After my first birth, I begged the kraamzorg not to leave. I was a wreck in so many ways and I just needed someone. She saw it in my eyes, and arranged with my midwife and huisart (GP) to stay almost a week longer. I was so thankful. She got me up and walking around outside and back to life."

"My kraam nurse was a huge help around the house, but even more important was how reassuring and empathetic she was in a difficult time. I needed that. She was a lifesaver."

Italian mom (living in NL)

Polish mom (living in NL)

"I needed a lot of help with breastfeeding and she (kraamzorg) was a pro. I couldn't have done it without her help. She was determined to make it happen—and it did!"

"My [kraamzorg] made me feel like the most important person in the world. She cooked delicious healthy food for us, helped with chores, and was so pleasant and respectful. I really feel like she was a gift from God."

American mom (living in NL)

Canadian mom (living in NL)

"Both times my kraamzorg nurse left (after the 8-10 days) I bawled my eyes out. They were so kind, and such a huge help. I could not have gotten through that first week without them."

97

Kraamvisite

The visiting of a new baby (and new parents) is somewhat of a social obligation in the Netherlands. This visit, called *kraamvisite*, or *kraambezoek*, usually occurs in the first few days or weeks of a baby's birth. As with most Dutch appointments, this one is usually scheduled in advance, either by contacting the new mother or father. The visit is normally relatively short and sweet, with the exchange of a baby gift and something small to eat and drink. This is also when the traditional Dutch *beschuit met muisjes* are served!

The visits are normally spread out over the first few weeks of a baby's arrival. For many mothers this can be an overwhelming or isolating time, and the Dutch system allows for contact, care, distraction, and companionship during what can be a difficult period.

I wasn't sure why the Dutch tradition of the kraamvisite had me so nervous. I wasn't a particularly private person, but the period after birth just seemed so unknown, so precious—and potentially overwhelming—that I didn't want to fill it up with agenda appointments.

A Dutch friend sent me a link to a popular Dutch website that contained all sorts of articles on having a baby.* One of the links she specifically mentioned in the message was a page of tips relating to the kraamvisite. "This should help explain it!" The article explained the importance of the visits and contained a list of instructions to help new mothers "avoid over-exertion and disappointing friends/family":

- ✔ Reserve the first day for close family only.
- ✔ Make sure to keep an agenda and schedule all visits.
- ✔ Maximum of two visits per day: one in the morning, one in the afternoon.
- ✔ Plan an hour of rest for yourself mid-day to relax.
- ✔ Keep it quiet—don't have too many small children running around your house.
- ✔ Keep it short: one-hour maximum.
- ✔ Keep it clean: ask visitors to always wash their hands.
- ✔ Ask for help: visitors are there to help you as well.
- ✔ Follow your feelings—if you feel like cancelling an appointment, do so, no one will mind.

Reading the article's practical tips, I felt even less convinced of its necessity. One of the things I found most frustrating about Dutch culture was the incessant scheduling of appointments and social events. The thought of now having to schedule my "after-baby" life made me slightly anxious! Every now and then, I feel an intense urge to rebel against Dutch culture. Perhaps it is a form of home-sickness, or a need to assert and embrace my "otherness." Regardless of the true cause, I forcefully closed the book and decided then and there that the Dutch *kraamvisite* was not for me. I'd have people over on my own terms, when and how I saw fit. After all, as the very practical Dutch article had kindly pointed out, "*er kunnen mensen op visite komen die je liever niet aan je bed wilt hebben*" (translation: There could be people coming to visit you'd rather not have on your bed!)—ain't nobody got time for that!

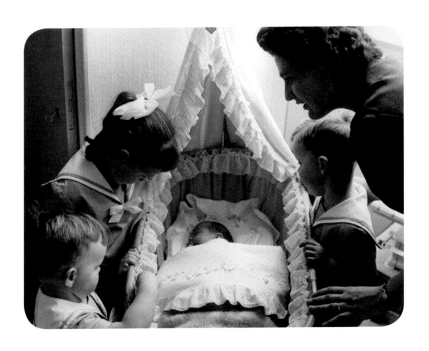

Thoughts on the Dutch *Kraamvisite*

"The kraamverzorgster *is really good at handling guests and visits. She made sure people only stayed as long as I could handle. And she kicked out a few early for me."*

Dutch mom

British mom (living in NL)

"This is one of the times I really felt foreign living here. I didn't like the idea of people visiting me so soon after birth, and I didn't think it was safe for a new baby to be exposed to so many people (and germs). My Dutch husband could not understand my reaction. I just did not want it. Eventually we decided on hosting people, all together, four weeks later. I guess it was a compromise."

Dutch mom

"The key to the kraamvisite *is having either your* kraamzorg *or husband manage the whole thing. My Dutch husband did it for me (as the nurse had already left when we started them). He made sure only two groups of people came each day and that they stayed for 20 minutes maximum. I just sat back and enjoyed the whole thing."*

"I waited four weeks, as I didn't want the pressure of a ton of people visiting me so soon after giving birth."

American mom

"I really didn't feel comfortable with so many people meeting and holding my newborn baby. In the Middle East (where we lived before moving here) they have almost the exact opposite tradition. There is a waiting period of a month or longer where no one other than the mother is allowed to hold the new baby. I was told this is to protect the baby from germs and infections. This is a tradition I could get behind!"

Dutch mom

Dutch mom

"I always gave everyone the tip that if you want friends and family to come later then you just have to send out the geboortekaart later. No one comes until they have received it, so you can buy some more time that way!"

"A kraamparty or kraamborrel is also possible. I did this for my second and third babies and found it much more enjoyable. You invite everyone over, three to four weeks after the birth for a short three-hour party."

Dutch mom

"I loved this Dutch tradition. It made me feel very special and loved. So many people wanted to come visit, and I was able to space the visits over many weeks, giving me a lot to look forward to!"

American mom

Consultatiebureau

The Dutch health system for children is centred around specialist health care centres, known as the *consultatiebureau*. These "well baby clinics" can be found throughout every city in the Netherlands. The centres offer regular appointments at scheduled intervals for the basic care of all children between the ages of 0-4 years old.

*"The Centre for Children and Families (*consultatiebureau*) provides information, advice and help with child development and parenting. It is a one-stop shop for children's health and wellbeing" (The Hague Center for Children & Families).*

After a child is born, the *kraamzorg* nurse arranges for the transfer of care to the *consultatiebureau*. The first visit, normally, takes place as a house-call, with nurses visiting the new baby in his or her home. The nurse will check the baby's weight, see how feedings are going, and answer any additional questions or concerns. The first regular check-up at the *consultatiebureau* takes place when your baby is four weeks old. From this point onwards, a series of check-ups will be scheduled. An information hotline also exists if you have any questions about your child (up until the age of four years old) that you want to discuss with a nurse.

The services of the *consultatiebureau* are completely free, and although it is not mandatory by law to attend the visits, the vast majority of Dutch parents do so. Most appointments are conducted by either a medical doctor or a nurse, depending on the nature of the appointment. At each appointment, the medical staff check the child's development (height, weight, growth, measurements, eyes, reflexes, etc.) as well as provide information on your child's care in accordance to their age and specific needs. The national vaccination program is also carried out by the *consultatiebureau* and vaccines are administered during these appointments.

The appointments are not to be confused with a regular doctor appointment. This is not the place you would call or visit if your child is ill. Those responsibilities are still cared for by your *huisarts* (general practitioner).

Similar to the care during pregnancy and after birth, the system is supported by yet another book in the *Groeiboek* series. You will recall from the previous chapters there were individual books for "Pregnancy," "Breastfeeding," and "Post-natal care."

"The role of the juvenile health care programme is to monitor children's development, maintain preventative health care and stimulate a healthy lifestyle. A healthy start in life is key to a happy childhood. You will naturally have many questions during your child's early years. During a visit to the consultatiebureau, your child's growth and development will be routinely checked from birth until he starts primary school at the age of 4. From practical tips to important vaccinations, the centre is there for children and their parents" (The Hague Center for Children & Families).

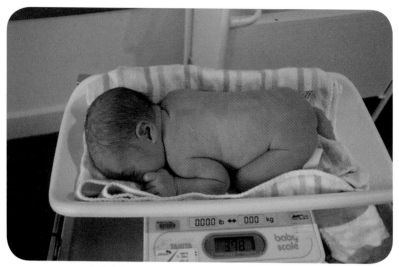

Baby's first appointment at the consultatiebureau

Charting the baby's growth

The consultatiebureau *will chart your baby's development. This will all be recorded in the so-called 'Groeiboekje' (Growth Book). The growth book outlines a baby's first year of development, supplies important phone numbers, holds your appointments at the clinic, records vaccinations, and charts your baby's height and weight. You should always bring this book with you to your appointments. (The Hague Center for Children & Families).*

What has always impressed me about the *consultatiebureau* is the organisation of the entire system. I found it was incredibly convenient to schedule appointments well in advance, receive a text message alert a few days prior, and know exactly what was to happen on a particular appointment date. In my experience, the staff were always quite knowledgeable and open to differing perspectives—of course, such situations always depend on the nurse or doctor whose care you are under, but my personal experience has been nothing but positive.

I also found these "well child" visits rather refreshing. It was a luxury to bring a new baby to an appointment without worrying about exposing them to a waiting room full of sick children and adults.

"I like the idea of separating wellness visits from sick visits. One is scheduled and focused on normal development while the other one is unpredictable and hopefully less frequent."

American mom (living in NL)

"I have mixed feelings about the consultatiebureau. It is nice to know if things go well with your kid, but it also feels a bit invasive."

Dutch mom

"I love the consultatiebureau. I'm serious. I really do—an incredible service and resource for parents."146

American mom (living in NL)

"I think the CB's role in checking your child's physical development is very good. But their advice (how much a kid should drink, when to start solid foods, etc.) was not for me. Every child is different. And as a parent I think you know what is best for your kid."

Dutch mom

American mom (living in NL)

"I don't use them as a resource. I use the Internet and friends and if there is something concerning, I'll seek a specialist. I do think the program and structure is helpful to keep me on track with check-ups, etc."

"I found the CB enormously useful. I never had to keep track of vaccinations schedules. I always knew I could call them with questions, concerns, to ask for advice, etc. They were always professional, punctual, and polite. The locations were safe and clean. My children were always treated kindly and felt comfortable. It was all FREE! I am aware that some people are uncomfortable with the government being so involved in the healthcare of private citizens. I know people personally who have had negative experiences with their local CB. But based on my own experiences and personal views on public health, I'm definitely a big fan!"

American mom (living in NL)

"I liked having a reference for my children's weight, height, and general development. I also found the CB useful if you and your husband have different opinions on parenting—nice to have a third point of view!"

Dutch mom

British mom (living in NL)

"I've always found the consultatiebureau really thorough in checking my kids' health and development. I appreciate always seeing the same paediatricians, unlike in London where the care is less personal. The only downside has been at times slightly over zealous assessment and measurement, such as about weight (too high and too low for each of my children) and not looking holistically at the child."

CHAPTER 5

BACK TO WORK
(WELL, SORTA...)

Y ou will have noticed that the vast majority of my observations on being a mother in the Netherlands have been very positive. However, when it comes to maternity leave policies, the Dutch unfortunately still have a long, *long* way to go. Maternity leave in the Netherlands is a dismal 16 weeks! For a country with such a progressive and female-friendly maternity culture, it was a shock to learn this—especially coming from Canada, where paid maternity leave can be up to a year long. Prior to living in the Netherlands, I had naively assumed that the Dutch leave would be comparable to the policies found in Nordic or Scandinavian countries, which is definitely not the case!

Of course, the topic of maternity and parental leave in the Netherlands has additional layers of complexity due to the amount of flexibility presented to Dutch women upon their return to work. The prevalence of an accepted culture of part-time workers in the Netherlands allows for many women to return, albeit early, to the option of a reduced work week. It could be for this reason that the system has yet to change, as the options for women after their maternity leave are indeed far superior to those found in other countries (namely Canada or the U.S.).

Do happy women = happier mothers?

A slew of recent studies have shown Dutch women to be among the happiest in the world! These studies consistently rank the Netherlands as one of the top five countries where women are happiest. When taking a closer look at the "World Happiness Ranking" (worldhappiness.report), the Netherlands, overall, comes very close to the top—weighing in at the 7th happiest nation. In comparison, Canada beats out the Netherlands ever so slightly at the 6th spot. America, Germany, and the U.K. are found in the 13th, 16th, and 23rd spots, respectively.

Question: **Why are Dutch women happy?**

Answer: Because the Netherlands is a matriarchy and the women are in charge.

Dutch Father

Dutch Father

Question: **Why are Dutch men happy?**

Answer: Because the women told them to be.

Over the past decade, articles in the English-language media have focused on this "phenomena" and attempted to analyze how and why this was the case. 'Think' pieces in the *New York Times, Salon*, Canada's popular *Macleans'* Magazine and a host of other publications have all come up with similar conclusions: Dutch women appear to have it all, and having it all apparently does lead to happiness! The "all" in question is the elusive, yet ever so important balance between family life and work.

"Living in a wealthy, industrialized society plays a huge part in the Dutch woman's sense of contentment, [says author Ellen de Bruin], given the benefits of a social net that allows for balance between work and family life. She backs that claim with statistics: 68 percent of Dutch women work part time, roughly 25 hours a week, and most probably do not want a full-time job" (New York Times "Why Dutch women don't get depressed").

Let's jump in and take a closer look at why Dutch women are so darn happy and how the Dutch systems allows for moms to have it all!

In this chapter

- Maternity leave
- Parental leave
- Part-time work
- Daddy days
- *Oma and Opa*

Maternity leave

I am sure I am not the first foreigner to wrongly assume the Netherlands' maternity policies were more progressive and in line with the rest of Europe. Little did I know that the Netherlands actually comes very close to the bottom of the list with its dismal 16 weeks. Perhaps surprisingly, Bulgaria and Greece top the list, providing new mothers with 58.6 weeks (at 90% of gross income) and 43 weeks (at 50% of gross income) of paid maternity leave, according to recent figures from the OECD.

Although brief, the Dutch maternity leave is unique, as it is split into two distinct categories: pre-birth leave and post-birth leave.

Pre-birth leave:
- ranges between four and six weeks
- a Dutch mother-to-be must go on leave no later than four weeks prior to the expected due date
- a Dutch mother-to-be can go on leave as early as six weeks prior to the expected due date
- leave could be longer than six weeks if baby is overdue

Post-birth leave:
- ranges between ten and twelve weeks
- starts the day after delivery

Splitting the leave into these two specific periods is distinctly different than other countries, and ensures that working mothers-to-be are not racing into their labours exhausted and overworked.

The Dutch system essentially forces women to stop all paid work a minimum of four weeks prior to their due dates—allowing for some much-needed rest and decompression.

When first discussing this notion with friends of mine in Canada, most were surprised that the choice was not up to the pregnant woman to decide when she wanted to stop working. The North American system can inevitably put pressure on women to continue working up until the last minute. I had argued with a Canadian friend that there must be significant health benefits associated with stopping work earlier. She wasn't convinced, touting how she had worked up until three days before her labour, and had felt just fine, so we agreed to disagree.

Later that night, I turned to my trusty friend, Google, to see whether any data existed to support my hunch. Sure enough, a study published in the Journal of Labor Economics in 2012 made the bold conclusion: "Working after eight months of pregnancy may be just as harmful as smoking." More specifically, researchers found that the "health effects associated with mothers who worked in the late stages of pregnancy were equal to that of smoking while pregnant."

Once again, I realized the Dutch were onto something! There is much to be said about being well-rested and stress-free before baby's delivery!

Since the total maternity leave in the Netherlands is, on average, 16 paid weeks, this would have most Dutch women returning to work when their new babies are only 3 months old. Many Dutch women choose to tack on additional time with unused holiday days or unpaid leave (if their employer approves), but for most women this does not account for a much longer stay at home.

Not all Dutch policies are as archaic, however, as expectant mothers in the Netherlands are fully protected by law from dismissal. Employers in the Netherlands are not allowed to fire women whilst pregnant and mothers-to-be cannot be let go during their maternity leave or their first six weeks back at work.

WEEKS OF PAID MATERNITY LEAVE

AVERAGE PAYMENT RATE ACROSS PAID MATERNITY LEAVE (%)

70 60 50 40 30 20 10 0

0 10 20 30 40 50 60 70 80 90 100

Bulgaria
Greece
United Kingdom
Slovak Republic
Croatia
Czech Republic
Ireland
Poland
Hungary
Italy
Estonia
Chile
Denmark
Cyprus
Lithuania
Malta
Romania
OECD average
Finland
Canada
Austria
France
Luxembourg
Netherlands
New Zealand
Spain
Turkey
Latvia
Belgium
Slovenia
Germany
Israel
Japan
Switzerland
Iceland
Norway
Korea
Mexico
Sweden
Australia
Portugal
United States

Source: OECD "*Key Statistics of Parental Leave Systems*" (2016)

160 140 120 100 80 60 40 20 0   0 10 20 30 40 50 60 70 80 90 100

Estonia
Finland
Hungary
Slovak Republic
Czech Republic
Norway
Latvia
Korea
Bulgaria
Sweden
Austria
Germany
Japan
Lithuania
Romania
Slovenia
OECD average
Canada
Denmark
France
Italy
Luxembourg
Poland
Croatia
Portugal
Belgium
Iceland
Australia
Chile
Greece
Ireland
Israel
Mexico
Netherlands
New Zealand
Spain
Switzerland
Turkey
United Kingdom
United States
Cyprus
Malta

Source: OECD *"Key Statistics of Parental Leave Systems"* (2016)

What do moms think of Dutch maternity leave?

Dutch mom

"Sixteen weeks?!? If they want to motivate women to work more, they should learn from the Scandinavians. Sixteen weeks is far too short! That first year is everything. For mom, dad, and baby!"

"Maternity leave really needs to change. It needs to be much longer—also for the dads."

Dutch mom

Swedish mom (living in NL)

"The Netherlands has a long way to go with their policies for working mothers. The only way the process will improve is if we have stronger representation by females in politics who make it a priority in this country. It is the only hope for change."

"My friends and family back home just assumed I would have an excellent (maternity) leave living in Europe! I had to tell them that not all European countries are the same—16 weeks is really too short. Of course, the American policy is not great either—but I would expect more from the Netherlands."

American mom (living in NL)

"This makes me really angry! What is our government telling us? That we are not valuable employees? That we should just quit if we want more time with our babies? Are they expecting us to pay our entire salary (or a very large portion of it) to daycare?!"

Dutch mom

Dutch mom

"I think the only real solution is that we, as women, actively involve ourselves more in politics and policy-making."

Dutch mom

"This is why I decided to not go back to work. The current situation does not work for many women. Things need to change."

"I decided to give up my full-time job to be with my daughter because the math did not add up. I thought four months was too early to leave her at daycare all day and my entire salary was basically paying for daycare. Of course, this was best for our family—whatever works for you!"

British mom (living in NL)

American mom

"16 weeks? This would be a luxury in the States. I guess it's all relative!"

Parental leave

Dutch parents do, however, have an added bonus: parental leave (*ouderschapsverlof*). All parents in the Netherlands (mothers or fathers), who have worked for the same employer for at least one year, are entitled to an unpaid parental leave to care for children under the age of eight. Dutch parents are entitled to leave up to 26 times of their weekly working hours.

For example:
an employee who works 32 hours per week would be entitled to 26 X 32 = 832 hours, in total, of parental leave.

Many parents choose to take this leave by working half their hours for an extended period, or working 1-2 fewer days per week. Others decide to take it all at once.

Although parental leave is unpaid, it allows Dutch mothers and fathers to work a reduced workload in order to spend more time with their children, without jeopardizing or having to forsake their current position. Some employees are fortunate enough to have their employers cover a portion of their leave as well, although this is not the norm.

I know many mothers in the Netherlands who have taken advantage of this leave in order to spend more time with their children and families during the very busy years of early childhood. Of those I spoke to, the guarantee of returning to their same job, or maintaining their current position was paramount. The Dutch have found a simple and cost-effective way to ensure Dutch moms do not need to choose between their careers or their family, allowing moms to take one step further towards "having it all."

Although parental leave is available for both Dutch moms and Dutch dads, the Centraal Bureau voor de Statistiek (CBS) reported that in 2013 more than three-quarters of fathers chose to not take parental leave. More specifically, 23.4% of fathers took the leave, compared to 57% of mothers.

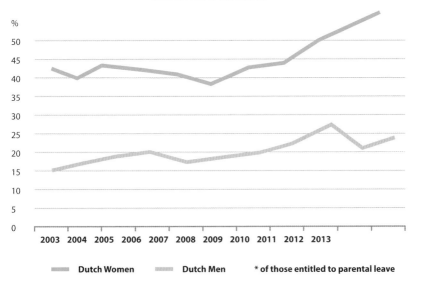

% Of Dutch Parents Who Have Made
Use Of Parental Leave*

Dutch Women   Dutch Men   * of those entitled to parental leave

Overall, parental leave in the Netherlands has been steadily on the rise for the past decade. As with most voluntary work leaves, the more commonplace and accepted they become, the more mothers and fathers will feel confident taking advantage of them!

Part-time work

The Dutch are known for their culture of part-time work. It is not unusual in the Netherlands for a man or woman to work a reduced work week, or work a full week condensed into four days. The Dutch, in fact, work the fewest hours of any other nation in the European Union. Employees in the EU work an average of 37.5 hours a week; whereas the Dutch, in comparison, work a mere 30.6 hours— nearly one full work day less per week! (*RNW*, "Dutch workers are efficient, not lazy")

When comparing the average Dutch working hours (30.6hrs/week) to those of a North American worker (44–52hrs/week), the variance is even more startling! Crunch the numbers and you will find that it amounts to a minimum of 87 fewer working days per year between the Dutch and the Americans! Quite a substantial difference!

Interestingly enough, the Dutch still manage to top the productivity list in the EU (*Guardian*, "Who works the longest hours in Europe?"), proving that a reduction in working hours and a sizeable part-time workforce does not necessarily correlate to reduced output. This leaves the remaining question: What is stopping other nations from following the Dutch lead?

"Off to work!"

Who doesn't like working less?

"Many Dutch people work part-time, for different reasons. Some prefer this because they want to spend more time with their kids or enjoy a healthier work/ life balance."

Dutch dad

Dutch mom

"Many Dutch people work part-time, because we don't live to work, we work to live."

"Dutch people are just SMART: work less, enjoy more, and be the most productive country at the same time!"

Dutch dad

Dutch woman

"Productivity doesn't come in hours, it is how you spend those hours. Work hard (efficient), play hard. What could be better?! All this free time is also good for the economy. More time for shopping, sport clubs, drinking a cup of coffee, a glass of wine on a terrace, etc."

American dad

"Here in the U.S., it is clear that most dads would like to be more involved than they are, but are prevented from doing so based on workplace and societal expectations (there's tons of research to demonstrate this). More flexible work options would be a great start."

"My wife works a full 36 hours a week, though she fits it into four days! Now that's clever!"

Dutch dad

Dutch dad

"There are plenty of men who also work only four days. It's not entirely socially accepted, unfortunately. I've turned down jobs because they insisted on five days, but I really want to spend that extra day with my son. But my brother and various childless friends also work four days. Whenever a prospective employer refuses my four-day work week, I ask why, and often they don't really know either."

American mom

"I think this is a marvellous idea. We here in America are a working society and our children are suffering from that. Families are dissolving and becoming obsolete. We have lost our priorities–like making our families come first and we are suffering for it. I admire the Dutch. If only we could learn from the Dutch and change our values, we could become a better and safer place to live."

Generous holidays

In addition to shorter work weeks, Dutch employees are entitled to four times the number of days they work per week in paid vacation days.

For example:

an employee in a five-day per week contract would be entitled to 20 days of annual paid leave, each year.

Many Dutch employers offer additional holiday days, or the possibility to 'save up' overtime hours. If this all sounds too good to be true, wait—we've got even more good news! In the spring of each year, Dutch employees have another treat: holiday pay! All employees in the Netherlands are entitled to a bonus 8% pay-out, per year, on their gross incomes. Known as 'holiday pay', most companies pay out this allowance just prior to the kick-off of summer holidays in May.

Whether it's paid holiday time, extra cash for a vacation, or reduced working hours, the Dutch certainly *seem to have managed to have their cake* and eat it too!

Family-centric work policies

The Dutch school system also favours a part-time working climate, as school hours in the Netherlands can often cause scheduling difficulties for families with two full-time working parents. School finishes by 15:00, and on Wednesdays children attend school only in the morning. This makes things less than conducive for the daily juggle of parenthood and full-time work. You will,

Dutch vs American holiday policies:

"You have statutory rights to work part-time in the Netherlands that do not exist in the U.S. Also, our medical insurance is often tied to our working full-time. The U.S. has no statutory requirements on how many hours worked, how many holidays or vacation days guaranteed off, or paid sick leave. And yes, many partners BOTH work just to pay the bills, with one of them desperate to keep a job with health insurance. I tried for years to work part-time here in the U.S. when my children were younger only to be told that I could not—I had to quit or work full-time."

American mom

Dutch woman (living in America)

"Living as a Dutch person in the U.S. and moving here after my 30th [birthday], I had to make a huge adjustment. Mandatory overtime, are you kidding me?! Making me come in on my day off to work. Yes, you'll pay me time and a half, but I'd rather use my personal time differently. When I explain to my American co-workers about the Dutch vacation days, they are AMAZED!"

Dutch man

"Don't forget about Dutch vacation pay! When that deposit comes in your bank account in May, it is always a beautiful surprise! Yippee —holiday time!"

"I left NYC to marry a Dutch person. Since I've been working in the Netherlands, I work far fewer hours (32) than NYC (50), and have 15x the money in the bank. I barely work! The Dutch expect you to have a life outside of work, which is lovely. The downside is all of these part-time workers are only available a few days a week and things that could be attended to quickly or resolved quite easily get tossed by the wayside or forgotten. I don't see this as efficient at all. I really miss that . . . but then I remember that I get paid tons of money and have five weeks of vacation, so I suck it up!"

American woman (moved to NL)

Dutch man

"Our system of 'flex-time' even allows us to get extra vacation days! When starting a job, you get the standard 20 working days of vacation. For every two years working for the company, you get an extra day. This means that after ten years, you get 25 days of paid vacation per year. That's two weeks in the summer and two weeks in the winter. Plus, five days to be spread over half working days whenever you need them. Also when temperatures reach 30 degrees Celsius you leave at 2 pm."

however, typically find parents in the Netherlands taking Wednesday off, to fetch, care, and spend time with their children!

Among those of us foreign to the Netherlands many wonder whether the system was built as a result of the Dutch part-time working culture, or if it in fact had helped create or maintain it! *Did Dutch parents need to work less because the schools hours were inconvenient, or were the school hours a result of so many Dutch parents choosing to work less?* A "chicken and egg" conundrum of sorts, to which I imagine there is no clear answer.

I strongly believe that the Dutch part-time work culture hugely benefits families—especially those with small children—in countless immeasurable ways. Having the opportunity for flexibility in your work week is invaluable when raising children. Ultimately, it allows for a much better balance within a family and inevitably leads to Dutch parents spending more time with their children.

Is part-time work the "norm" for Dutch women?

The Dutch have been long praised for their impressive work-life balance. Dutch women, however, appear to have the sweetest deal of all, with many women happily choosing to work part-time, and a great many mothers choosing to do so after having children.

I recently realized that, of all the Dutch mothers I personally know, I did not know a single example of one working a full-time work week! Although anecdotal evidence (and partially skewed due to my work in the governmental sector), it does give an indication of the prevalence and desirability of part-time work for mothers in the Netherlands.

According to the latest official national statistics (CBS, 2014), my circle of friends does not exactly represent all Dutch working mothers, but it is also not too far from the truth. One in three Dutch women "stop working or work less" after the birth of their first child, and a mere 12% of working Dutch mothers (with children under 18 years old) work "full-time" (i.e. more than 35 hours per week). This would account for roughly one in eight Dutch mothers holding down a full-time job. (It seems as though I need an eighth Dutch mother as a friend, although I would imagine if she was working full-time, she might be too busy to befriend me…)

As an outsider, I truly believe Dutch mothers come pretty close to "having it all." Although maternity leave is not nearly long enough, the acceptance of part-time work (even at higher levels) allows for many women to not have to make the exceedingly difficult decision between being either a "stay-at-home mom" or a "working mom." The system in many other countries, and certainly

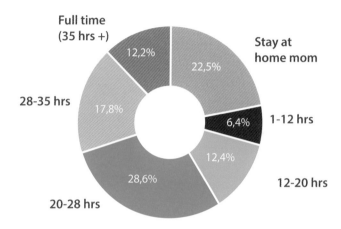

Weekly Working Hours of Dutch Mothers
(with children under the age of 18)

Source: CBS (2014).

in Canada and the U.S., often forces women to choose between those two options. *Why can't we have the opportunity to do and be both? And why shouldn't we?* It appears the Dutch have figured out what we all inherently know is true: working less is simply better!

Dutch moms weigh in on part-time work

Dutch mom

"Whoever said that being a mama or papa part of the week and actually raising your children instead of taking them full-time to daycare centres, or caring for elderly parents, is easier than working? It is more satisfying, though . . . and didn't I read somewhere that Dutch children are among the most relaxed and happy?"

Dutch mom

"Working part-time is not always a free choice. There can be several reasons: 1) The amount of money spent for childcare is often almost as much as a woman would earn, especially if there is more than one kid. 2) Most women have the freedom to work part-time, because the financial space in their household is there. 3) Many jobs are often only available part time. 4) A lot of women's jobs are so incredibly badly paid, it is almost a hobby; and once the children are born, most hobbies disappear."

Portuguese mom

"I'm Portuguese, living in the Netherlands, and I've never had so much quality of life, and I guess that's because (finally) I learned how to 'not work' just like the Dutch do."

"I read an article by an American lady once who thought that all Dutch women spend their days drinking coffee instead of having a career. It just pissed me off . . . Although a lot of Dutch women work part-time, to compare this with America is just not right, because I think that in America you have: 'stay-at-home mums' or 'career women' and very few women who work part-time. I really don't know a lot of strictly 'stay-at-home mums' among my Dutch friends, but a lot of friends who are mums do work part-time."

Dutch mom

Dutch mom

"I work part-time; that's a personal choice. I enjoy it—I feel my life is more balanced. But when people tell me: "Oh boy, I wished I worked your hours; that would be easy," I kindly remind them that I also make way less money than they do. That silences people!"

Daddy-Day

A few years ago, an American friend of mine came to visit, so I took some time off to show her around Amsterdam. After a couple of hours wandering around the city, she suddenly stopped and blurted out, "What's going on in this town? Is there some sort of 'sexy single dad' convention on today?" I stared at her, utterly confused. "Come on!" she said. "What's with all the dads alone with their kids?" she exclaimed.

I looked around, fearing I had missed some parade of shirtless baby-wearing men marching down the street. Nothing was amiss; everyday scenes of Amsterdam life swirled around us. She went on to loudly express her utter amazement at the number of "active" fathers she had seen alone (gasp!) with their children around town that day. "Remember that dad this morning riding the bike with his three kids? And all those dads we passed in the park ... and now that dad over there feeding a baby, and that guy pushing the stroller, and that one by the canal ..."

I cut her off, as clearly this exercise could go on all day, and her finger-pointing and elevated voice was starting to attract a few pairs of curious eyes. "Shhhh," I replied. "They're just all on their "papadag!" I should have guessed this wouldn't quiet her down: "Their WHAT??" she cried.

The Dutch word *papadag* doesn't have me bat an eyelid now, but back when I first arrived in the Netherlands my reaction was pretty similar to my Canadian friends. *What? Men take a day off work, EVERY week, to just be with their children?!* It wasn't that the concept itself wasn't appreciated, it was just so utterly unheard of. In North America, a day off *each month* for fatherly duties would be a shocker, let alone a day a week!

According to national statistics, over a third of men in the Netherlands work a reduced work week and a sizeable 15% of fathers choose to work a reduced week (CBS). In a recent poll carried out by the CBS, an astounding 66% of young men said they planned to reduce their working hours when they became a father. Whether or not this will be possible, financially or otherwise, for such a high number of men will remain to be seen; however, this figure illustrates a major desire of Dutch males to actively participate in child-rearing and weekly childcare duties.

Many Dutch employers are accustomed to the "daddy-day" arrangement and some even offer it as a selling point in interviews or contract negotiations. It does help that, according to the *Economist*, the Netherlands has a "rather laid-back approach to work: with more than half of the Dutch working population working part-time, a far greater share than in any other rich-world country."

The New York Times ran a feature article entitled "Working (Part-Time) in the 21st Century" and introduced America to the concept of the Dutch "daddy day":

> *"'Working four days a week is now the rule rather than the exception among my friends,' said Mr. Vermaire, the first man at Wijn & Stael Advocaten to take a 'daddy day' in 2006. Within a year, all the other male lawyers with small children in his firm had followed suit."*

I believe it is truly a privilege to live in a nation where men not only have the desire, but also the opportunity, to actively participate in weekly child care duties. Many Dutch parents may take this as a given, but it is entirely not the case in other countries.

A recent study in America attempted to gauge the opinions of employers regarding men and deliberate part-time work choice.

The study concluded that men were more likely to be penalized for working part-time than women: "Part-time work arose in the U.S. economy as heavily feminized types of work. Employers might perceive nonstandard employment histories as a common experience for women. For men, by contrast, employers may take such a history as a signal that the male worker was unable to find a full-time, standard job."(David Pedulla, *Penalized or Protected? Gender and the Consequences of Nonstandard and Mismatched Employment Histories*)

One thing is true, though: if you spend any time in the Netherlands, you are sure to see dads playing an active role in parenting. This equation, of course, is good for the entire family. In households where fathers are more active in parenting, wives and mothers are happier too. Dutch "daddy days" are as beneficial for the moms as they are for the dads!

Thoughts on the Dutch concept of "Daddy days"

Dutch mom

"I didn't know it was this special! But a decade ago, 'daddy day' wasn't a common thing; until then, only women worked part-time. Now my husband works four days and I work three. So the kids are really always with one of their parents. When they get a bit older we can have weekends off together, but until then I rather like this solution."

"My American husband changed jobs to be home more with our special needs kids. He works evenings now, goes to work at 4pm. It's been lovely for all of us. We have less money, but that's okay. The kids are thriving having dad home for dinner (we have dinner at 3:30 . . . and that's okay, too!)."

Dutch mom

American dad

"I admire this notion: take a day off of work, just to spend with your kids, and do it often."

142

Dutch mom

"I love the concept of 'daddy days'! My American mom-in-law was shocked too, to see how many dads took and fetched kids from school!"

"My husband always took a 'daddy day' when the kids were young. He is a director, with a very good job, but he made a point to do so, so that others would feel like they could also! (And of course he enjoyed it too!)"

American mom (in NL)

"We used to live in the Netherlands and got very used to this. It was a big shock moving to America with my Dutch husband, and him having to be at work ALL the time. No more papadag! At least he had the time with the kids at home when they were little."

American mom

Canadian mom

"Oh, how I wish this was possible here in Canada. My husband tried to ask for a similar arrangement but it was flat-out refused. I think things are changing . . . but slowly."

Dutch mom

"A dad who chooses to have a 'daddy day' has either chosen to work less—which means less money—or arranges his work hours to have a day off. This is easier if you have a flexible schedule or a 36-hour work week. The truth is that this isn't possible for many parents and more women will work less to be at home more."

"I love the idea of papadag; on my countless trips to the Netherlands I have often seen papas and opas alone with their children or grandchildren, cycling around the city or at the market or in the park. It is a great concept that should be adopted globally."

American dad

145

"I work four days of nine hours each and truly enjoy my Fridays off with my son."

Dutch dad

"Unfortunately, not every Dutch family can afford to work a day less every week. Also not every kind of profession or boss is willing to give one day off every week, which is a shame!"

Dutch dad

"Going to the zoo again tomorrow! Love my 'daddy day' . . . still work 60 hours a week, so this is the best time off for me."

Dutch dad

"I hope that this can be a reality for all Dutch dads. It does seem to me that it is a luxury for mostly the middle and upper class. I hope that changes."

Dutch dad

"I moved to the Netherlands a few years ago from the U.K. I find the whole papadag thing pretty normal now—most of my friends in the neighbourhood work part-time, and it's nice to meet other dads on papadag.

British dad (in NL)

Oma and *Opa*

Let's not forget beloved *oma* and *opa*! Dutch grandparents play a significant role in childcare in the Netherlands. Aside from *papadag* and *mamadag,* many Dutch grandparents also have a fixed day each week where they look after their grandchildren. I must say, I've always been impressed seeing such spritely seniors chasing toddlers or biking around Amsterdam with babies in tow!

My hunch was that Dutch grandparents lessened the load substantially for Dutch parents; however, I was pleased to have this confirmed by a recent report on parenting in the Netherlands. It turns out, Dutch grandparents are amongst the most involved in Europe!

> *"Not only do 65% or more of Dutch grandmothers provide at least some childcare but so do about 60% of grandfathers" (Diederik F. Janssen, Rutgers, "State of World's Fathers," Country Report: Netherlands).*

The necessity of grandparental care may be a result of rising daycare costs in the Netherlands—and interestingly, may also be a leading factor in Dutch parents' decision to have additional children. Data from the Netherlands' Kinship Panel Study found that "involvement of both maternal and paternal grandparents increased the likelihood of additional births." Thinking of having more children? Turns out, it may be handy to snag yourself a Dutch *oma* (or *opa*)! And we kid you not, several Dutch "adopt-an-oma" services exist!

"When I first got pregnant my Dutch mother-in-law said: Baby can be one day a week with me! she now also does an extra day, every second week!"

Dutch mom

Dutch mom

"My mom always said (before I got pregnant) that she didn't want to be tied down for a specific day every week. But when she became a grandma she changed her mid (maybe a bit of grandma competition going on!)"

"In our house, Wednesday is mamadag (I stay home with the kids), Friday is papadag (husband stays home), and Monday is omadag (grandma stays home)!"

Dutch mom

"Boy, we could learn so much from this. The Dutch really have it right, don't they?!"

American mom

CHAPTER 6

THE THREE "R'S": THE WISDOM OF DUTCH GRANDMOTHERS

Peace, purity, and regularity. If these three pillars of Dutch parenting sound rather old-fashioned, it's because they are. Known in the Netherlands as the "*Drie R's*" (Three R's), they are said to have been touted as the key to Dutch parenthood from as early as the 1900s.

The exact origin of the Three R's has been debated. It has been said that they are based on principles touted by Florence Nightingale in her 1859 book *Notes on Nursing*. Nightingale's guiding principles (the need for fresh air, light, variety, nourishing food, peace and quiet) concerned general health and the care of hospital patients. How they became synonymous with parenting and childcare in the Netherlands is anyone's guess! Others claim they did not come from Nightingale at all, but were rather a distillation of the prevailing Calvinistic values of the time.

Regardless of their exact origins, much has been noted about the Three R's and the importance they play in parenting in the Netherlands. Starting in the early 1900s the Dutch *consultatiebureau* instructed new mothers on the importance of adhering to the Three R's and widely distributed a flyer under the same name.

Throughout the 1940s and 1950s, these principles continued to set the standards for Dutch mothers and caregivers. In fact, during these two decades, the Three R's were so widely revered that they graced the pages of nearly every Dutch textbook covering childcare and early childhood education. Doctors, nurses, and childcare workers cited the Three R's as the perfect formula for child-rearing and the antidote to unhappy and unruly babies.

The Three R's went out of style, for the most part, in the '60s and '70s when an anti-authoritarian wave swept Europe. However, they never fully disappeared

School voor Opleiding v. Leerkrechten
in Kinderverzorging en Opvoeding
te ROTTERDAM

GROENE EN WITTE KRUISGESCHRIFTJES, No. 9.

REINHEID, RUST EN
REGELMAAT

ZESDE   VIERDE

DRUK   10.000-TAL

EEN BEKNOPTE UITEENZETTING, HOE MOEDERS
HARE ZUIGELINGEN OP DE MINST OMSLACHTIGE
— WIJZE GOED KUNNEN VERZORGEN —

DOOR

A. G. VAN HULST

OUD-WIJKVERPLEEGSTER VAN DE VEREENIGING
„HET GROENE KRUIS" TE HARLINGEN.

Uitgave der Algemeene Nederlandsche Vereeniging „Het Groene
Kruis", verkrijgbaar aan het Centraal-Bureau dier Vereeniging,
Prinsegracht 126 te 's Gravenhage, tegen den volgenden prijs:
voor Nederland: f 0,15 per stuk, en (voor verspreiding) f 3.—
per 100; voor België: fr. 0.30 per stuk, en fr. 7.— per 100,
franco toegezonden.

's GRAVENHAGE 1916.

Flyer on parenting from 1916 entitled "Reinheid, Rust and Regelmaat"—
distributed by the *Consultatiebureau*.

153

from the Dutch parenting vernacular and in recent decades have continued to pop up in parenting magazines, websites, books, and research journals, as well as various publications—a true testament to their timeless nature.

So what exactly do the Three R's mean?

Translating the Three R's requires an understanding of Dutch culture and values, as well as insight into their application. Although the direct dictionary translation for the trio is "Peace, Purity, and Regularity," they could be more broadly interpreted as:

- *Rust*: (peace) calm, tranquillity, rest

- *Reinheid*: (purity) cleanliness, hygiene

- *Regelmaat*: (regularity) routine, consistency

The Three R's in practice

At one of my first appointments at the consultatiebureau, the Dutch nurse we were seeing quickly cited the Three R's in our discussion on babies and sleep training. This being the first time I had heard of them, I was curious to learn more and questioned her further on their exact meanings. She spoke of the importance of a peaceful and relaxed home (Rust); good hygiene, bathing routines, and healthy feeding (Reinheid); as well as the need for consistent feeding and sleeping routines (Regelmaat). I found the advice at the time to be both somewhat obvious and a little old-fashioned, yet in actual practice very effective.

What I find most interesting is that, although many Dutch mothers nowadays are not familiar with the Three R's by name, their guiding principles are still very much a part of the fundamentals of Dutch parenting. Whether or not they know the trio by name seems of little relevance. Many Dutch mothers I have spoken with or observed have cited both *rust* and *regelmaat* as key pillars in their parenting—with the vast majority following a set daytime and night-time schedule.

The application and interpretation of the Three R's, from the time of Dutch *omas* to modern-day Dutch mothers, can be roughly summarized as follows:

Rust: (peace) calm, tranquillity, rest
- sufficient sleep for baby and child
- the importance of a quiet and peaceful household environment
- necessary periods of mental calm and rest for baby and child
- avoiding excessive stimulation
- importance of peaceful and calm parenting

Reinheid: (purity) cleanliness, hygiene
- taking adequate care of a baby and child's physical needs importance of a safe and hygienic environment

Regelmaat: (regularity) routine, consistency
- the importance of predictability
- the importance of a regular, well-scheduled routine
- bedtime rituals (ex: bath, reading, lights-out)
- consistent morning wake-up times, as well as bedtimes
- consistent feeding schedule
- consistent boundaries and discipline

Advice from an official Dutch brochure from the "Centre for Youth & Families" (GGD—*Centrum voor jeugd en gezin*) in Groningen, 2016:

Rest and regularity for a fussy baby

Rust, Reinheid, and *Regelmaat.* Half a century ago these Three R's were very well known to young parents. Today we live in an increasingly busy and changing world; however, it is still highly advisable that parents ensure *rust* and *regelmaat*—especially for fussy babies.

The following is a list of tips that may help:

- A healthy balance of waking and sleeping.
- Create a calm environment (for example: where TV and electronics are limited).
- Minimize the amount of outings with the baby to ensure a proper sleep rhythm is maintained.

"It is very important that your child feels safe and secure, and we believe that the 3 R's (calm, cleanliness and regularity) play an important role in this. Especially for babies, we believe routine is essential. We follow a regular routine of resting, feeding times, play times, cuddle time and attention, this ensures a consistent and familiar day for your child" **(quote from a Dutch daycare center's website, 2016).**

- Ensure that you carry out a daily routine in the same manner, each day. For example, wake time, feeding, changing, playtime, and in bed at the first signs of fatigue.
- Baby-wearing and rocking give an infant comfort and necessary body contact.
- Babies sleep best in their own space/bed. The crib can be in the parents' room or a separate room.
- The playpen (box) is a place for the baby to learn to play alone.

And the research to prove it …

Sara Harkness and her husband Charles Super (both professors of Human Development and Family Studies at the University of Connecticut) have spent decades observing, researching, and analysing parental attitudes and beliefs across cultures. They have written dozens of publications on the topic of parenting and culture, and have drawn many revelatory conclusions from observing and interviewing parents around the world.

Over the past two decades, they have devoted a great deal of time to the study of Dutch parenting beliefs and behaviours. I will admit that, when I first stumbled across one of their publications in a research journal, I was elated! I finally had the "scientific proof" to support my claims that the Dutch, whether they knew it or not, were heavily influenced by the principles of the Three R's— and in particular the notions of rest and routine, and that these routines might aid in producing happier, calmer babies.

*"We discovered the Three R's of Dutch child-rearing—*rust *(rest),* regelmaat *(regularity), and* reinheid *(cleanliness)—while doing research on how Dutch parents in a typical mid-sized town think about the development of their infants and children, and how these ideas guide the way they organize children's lives from day to day.*

"Many of the Dutch parents we interviewed seem to show a fine-tuned awareness of the allocation of time during the day, and in particular the importance of regularity and rest.

*"Parents focused a great deal of care and attention on providing adequate rest or sleep in a regularly scheduled day, with the goal of bringing up children who would be calm, cheerful, and self-regulated." (*Sara Harkness, et al., *"The Anthropology of Learning in Childhood" and "Themes and Variations: Parental Ethnotheories in Western Cultures")*

A return to the Three R's in modern Dutch parenting

It seems that the Three R's are still valued by the majority of Dutch parents. On a popular Dutch parenting website (J/M voor Ouders), a recent study cited the desire for a revival of the Dutch Three R's. According to the study, 63% of respondents "wholeheartedly" agreed to a return to the "Three commandments" of rust, reinheid, and regelmaat. Readers, however, interpreted the second R (reinheid) slightly differently than generations before

> *"In this article we make the case for a return of two out of the famous three R's: the R of Rust (calm) and the R of Regelmaat"* **(quote from an official Dutch *"Centre for Youth & Family"* website, 2016).**

them. They acknowledged the importance of hygiene and cleanliness, as well as purity in terms of food choices (i.e. healthy, organic, etc.) and the protection of children from exposure to unnecessary household or environmental chemicals and toxins (i.e. smoking, pesticides, preservatives, etc.). Other parents suggested updating the trio by replacing reinheid (purity) with either the Dutch word richting (direction) or respect (respect).

Whether or not the Three R's ever make a full resurgence is yet to be seen. However, as we can see from the following quotes, many Dutch—knowingly or not—seem to follow the advice of their Dutch omas from yesteryear!

Do all Dutch moms follow the Three R's?

"I do, actually, follow the R's with my children—and in that order—but I would add a fourth R: 'relax' (and in front of the others). You need to relax, listen to your child, and adapt to its pace, but at the same time follow your own flow."

Dutch mom

Dutch mom

"To be honest, this is the first time I have ever heard of this! Sounds like something my oma would say."

"The Dutch are big on following schedules. Have you ever looked outside after 18:00? Not a single kid on the street as they are all eating dinner and then right off to bed!"

American mom (living in NL)

Dutch mom

"Rust and regelmaat does wonders. I always tell all friends with new babies to make sure to give your baby plenty of rest and structure."

"The 'drie R's' were from my grandmother's generation, and I know my mother is also a fan of them. Did I actively set out to follow them? No. But I do believe in not over-exciting a baby and having a somewhat strict schedule that you follow every day."

Dutch mom

Dutch mom

"I have seen some mothers who follow the rules of the Three R's too closely. I think you have to take your baby's lead, sometimes a perfect routine is not possible. I do not believe in letting them cry to force a schedule on them."

American mom (living in NL)

"I have never heard of the Three R's before! My husband is Dutch and both of my children were born here! It does sound quite Dutch to me!"

"To me, the Three R's always sounded a bit old-fashioned. But I had a pretty nice routine with my baby and I was calm and relaxed, so I guess I did end up following them!"

Dutch
mom

"I followed the Three R's in a way, but sometimes your day goes different, just like life does.
I think kids also need to get used to that as well."

Dutch
mom

Canadian mom
(living in NL)

"I found that Dutch mothers all talk A LOT about the importance of being a calm parent and following routines. The Dutch moms I see always seem to be so organized and on quite strict bedtime routines. I will say I try to have a consistent schedule with my kids, but it doesn't come that natural to me!"

CHAPTER 7

DUTCH BABIES
SLEEP BETTER

was sitting on a terrace in Amsterdam enjoying a late summer dinner with my husband and our baby girl. It couldn't have been much later than 20:00, maybe 20:30, but as I glanced around the crowded square full of buzzing restaurants and terraces, I noticed that we were, in fact, the only table with a child—let alone a baby. This wasn't such a surprising sight, as I had gathered from most of my Dutch mom friends that their babies were normally well into dreamland by this hour. I will admit I have never been one for strict routines or early bedtimes, so putting our daughter to bed while the sun was still shining seemed unnecessary.

It should have come as no surprise when the Dutch woman sitting at the table next to me turned and loudly inquired, "What time does your baby go to sleep?" I hesitated to answer, as her tone was more accusatory than inquisitive, but I replied with a vague "fairly soon." This was clearly not a satisfying answer as the woman went on to explain she had a son who looked roughly the same age who was fast asleep at home. "He would never make it to this hour," she said. "He'd be an utter nightmare! Plus, he sleeps straight through the night so I wouldn't want that to change." We chatted a few minutes longer, and I came to see that she was not, in fact, judging me as I had initially assumed. She seemed genuinely interested in our daily routine but surprised to hear of our "alternative" schedule. She referenced a friend in Spain, and one in the Middle East who also "kept their kids up," but surmised it was more due to the heat than anything else. She then asked if I worked full-time. I told her I worked four days a week, but sometimes I wished I could be at home more. "That's why you keep her up," she said matter-of-factly. "Working-mother's guilt—you want to spend more time with her."

Having already lived in the Netherlands for over a half dozen years at this point, I classified her comment as "typically Dutch"… I won't lie, at the time it did rub me the wrong way. As we pushed Kaia home in our stroller through the canal-lined streets, I remember muttering to my husband that "a Canadian would have never taken such liberties. Who did she think she was?!" It was very direct—and could certainly be interpreted by some expats or foreigners as unnecessary or even down-right rude—but I knew the Dutch psyche well enough to understand it was not coming from a place of malice.

That evening as I lay in bed, I realized that what the Dutch woman on the terrace had said was true. It had never really dawned on me before, but I did keep our daughter up "late" (by Dutch standards) in order to spend more time with her (as a result she slept in much later in the morning —as did I—and so, our routine suited us all just fine). However, Kaia's resistance to bedtime and wakings throughout the night were also much more pronounced whenever I let any semblance of routine fly out the window. I thought she also had had a point when it came to routine and good sleeping habits (Kaia was nowhere near sleeping through the night!),

but I wasn't quite ready to admit that! Over the years, I had learned to accept good
ol' "Dutch directness" but the Dutch Three R's and the adherence to a strict sleep
schedule were not on my list, yet!

It's all about routine

With two babies born in the Netherlands and having known and observed
countless others, I feel confident in making the following claim: Dutch babies
sleep. Furthermore, they sleep better than their North American counterparts.
And (wait for it, here is the kicker) they are happier as a result. I hear you asking,
"could this be true? And if so, *please* share their secret!" No problem—let's jump
right in!

We know that Dutch parents—whether or not they call it by name—adhere
to the principles of the Three R's, namely those that concern routines, rest,
and sleep schedules. As mentioned in an earlier chapter, leading parenting
researcher Sara Harkness and Charles Super identified that Dutch parents, on
average, place high values on structure and daily routines. In the publication
Themes and Variations: Parental Ethnotheories in Western Cultures, Harkness and
her fellow researchers explored the Dutch adherence to routines and looked at
its positive effect on sleep behaviours.

"The key to the Dutch parents' success in achieving a good night's sleep for both
their child and themselves seems to lie in the second component of the 'three
R's' ethnotheory: regularity. Many parents stressed the importance of a regular
schedule, including a set time for both meals and bed."

Most noteworthy of all their observations was the finding that Dutch babies actually slept more than their American counterparts—and had fewer sleep issues! On average, they found that Dutch babies were sleeping a total of 15 hours per day, whereas American babies, in similar situations, slept on average only 13 hours per day. Having observed Dutch parents and their somewhat "strict" routines for many years, I did not find these results surprising. However, I am sure they would raise more than a few eyebrows across the Atlantic!

"It is noteworthy that the Dutch ethnotheory of infant sleep, and the caretaking practices that they described to foster it, apparently were more successful in averting children's sleep 'problems,' at least from the parents' perspective: these Dutch parents hardly mentioned having any problems getting their children to follow the desired schedule. In contrast, the American parents spoke frequently about their struggles to deal with babies and young children whose innate temperaments and developmental patterns militated against easy management at night."

Returning to work after Kaiden was born was a challenge. Although generally a healthy, happy baby, he had developed a pesky - yet persistent- habit of waking up 3-5 times on any given night. Being surrounded by several Dutch colleagues with babies the same age I had often felt like we lived in entirely different universes as they all seemed to experience only a fraction of the sleep issues we were going through.

One day, after a particularly bad night I came into the office exhausted and mentioned my problem with Kaiden to a few Dutch colleagues. One listened patiently, then said: "I think you are actually the problem, Colleen. Sure, he wants to drink all night, but that doesn't mean he has to or even should". This advice was not groundbreaking but a familiar matter-of-fact, no nonsense attitude that I had come to appreciate from the Dutch. It was in fact perfectly logical and the solution was pragmatic as always: stop feeding him, he'll sleep, you'll sleep and that will be that. My response was plagued by guilt and "what-ifs". What if he needs me? What if he needs the milk? What if he is lonely and feels abandoned? The Dutch mothers looked on, and scoffed: "He doesn't need the milk. He doesn't need the mid-night attention. He needs a mother who sleeps and functions. Period.". Did I take their advice? Eventually. Did I feel guilty in the process? Hugely. And more importantly: Did it work? Yep. Like. A. Charm.

Judging by the sheer amount of sleeping aids, products, books, and expert opinions touted in North America, it seems that all is not well on the sleeping front. Scan the "sleep" aisle of any baby store and you'll be bombarded with specially concocted pillows, white noise machines, crib gadgets, sleeping pods, swings, black-out blinds, lullaby players, fancy clocks, teddy bears, essential oils, and so on, and so forth!

We know that having a baby or child that does not sleep can have a potentially devastating impact on a parent's health, happiness, relationships, and even on their career. Could the solution to North America's million-dollar "baby sleep industry" be as simple as following a daily "Dutch routine"?

Thoughts on "Dutch routine"

Dutch opa

"Don't know how it is nowadays, but for this 63-year-old, it was definitely early to bed! I resented it sometimes but we did not have cranky, under-rested kids."

"Many people do not realize that a baby needs around 16-20 hours of sleep a day; if not, the result is an over-tired and restless baby! If you apply rust and regelmaat you will get the most out of your baby (and frankly, out of yourself and possibly the rest of your family). My daughter is a lot calmer and happier since I gave her a regular routine with plenty of down-time."

Dutch mom

Dutch mom

"My son sleeps well, eats well, and is very happy to play alone. I think you need, as parents, to teach them these things. These are important life skills!"

"Dutch moms are so organized and great with routine! And yes, this is coming from a German!"

German mom (living in NL)

"My children always followed a routine and are both very good sleepers. I often see exhausted parents who have to lie in bed with their baby (and sometimes older children!) until they fall asleep. These parents are always surprised at how easily my children always went and still go to sleep without crying—simply due to a fixed and recognizable routine. My kids are 4 and 7 years old and still go to bed happily every night."

Dutch mom

Dutch mom

"Sleep is very important for both baby and mother. Having a fixed routine and structure was very necessary for my babies—and me! I think it kept us all sane!"

Canadian mom (living in NL)

"I have always said that Dutch parents are doing something right because it seems like Dutch babies, toddlers, and kids sleep great. Of course there must be exceptions, but in my Dutch office I always seemed to be the only one with kids at home not sleeping through the nights. I spent a lot of time and energy trying to figure out what they did differently, and I really just think it comes down to Dutch mothers being a bit stricter and disciplined when it comes to sleep and sleep-training!"

"From day one I followed the advice of my kraamzorg nurse and my Dutch mother-in-law when it came to sleeping. They both taught me to make sure the baby had enough quality sleep (ex: in their own bed, dark room, quiet) and to have a consistent night routine. My Dutch kraam nurse suggested always following a routine in the exact same order at bedtime (ex: bath, diaper, sleep sack, cuddle, lights out) and making sure to put them to bed every night at the same time. I have two very good sleepers—and I don't think it is a coincidence!"

American mom (living in NL)

Well-rested babies = happier babies

> *"In Holland, only 9% of babies are considered "fussy." In the United States, that number is 19%. The difference, many believe, is in the routine. Dutch families begin a routine from day one. It lowers stress hormones for the mom, and, as a result, for the babies as well." (Mary Sheedy Kurcinka, Sleepless in America)*

Apart from being better sleepers, new research (2015) has also shown that Dutch babies laugh, smile, and like to cuddle more than their American counterparts. On top of their cuddly and contented nature, Dutch babies also demonstrated greater "expressions of happiness" and were, in fact, "easier to calm or soothe when upset" (Marie-Therese Walsh, *Dutch and American Babies' Temperamental Differences*).

What I find most interesting in this study is the possible explanation for the notable differences between Dutch and American babies.

"A cultural emphasis on cognitive stimulation may lead U.S. infants to be more active and aroused than their Dutch counterparts. American infants also demonstrated higher levels of fear, frustration, and sadness."

Anyone who has spent time around Dutch parents knows that flashcards, helicopter parenting, and the pursuit of over-stimulating activities for their children are not high on their list—and according to the various research, they shouldn't be! Dutch parenting style focuses on plenty of calm and restful

periods, which seem to have a profound impact on their baby's well-being—and ultimately their character!

The Dutch attitude towards "over-stimulated" babies

Dutch mom

"My Dutch mum always said, 'babies need regular sleep times—when they're asleep their brains grow.' I agree—overtired, over-stimulated, and overwrought babies struggle to thrive, and it doesn't make for happy mums, either. Turns out she was spot on—lots of brain development and cellular growth and repair takes place when sleeping, and it's important throughout life!"

"I was surprised how many of my Dutch mom friends regularly used their playpens (box) as a sort of mental 'time-out' place for their babies. They talked about how they needed 'down time.' I always thought this was a bit strange, but it seems to actually make a lot of sense!"

Canadian mom (living in NL)

"Having lived in the U.S. myself, I totally relate to this. The over-stimulation of children in America abhorred me."

Dutch mom

"Just spent a whole day one-on-one (papadag) with my daughter of ten months old, having a lot of fun. Crawling around together, cuddling, throwing her up in the air (and catching!!) and taking walks and running errands. The only cognitive stimulus she's getting from me is clapping hands, waving...and seeing other people and new things every day. It was a gezellige dag."

Dutch dad

"The American 'pursuit of stimulation' sounds horrible. It's more important to talk. Talk a bit to your baby during the day about what you are doing. Let babies be babies, don't wind them up like a tiger mom."

Dutch mom

"Moving here from the States was a positive move in my parenting. We were 'disturbingly laid back' on the playgrounds in Chicago and now we seem to be more on the neurotic end of the spectrum in NL. But seriously, other parents make parenting too stressful in the U.S."

American mom

CHAPTER 8

DUTCH PARENTING FUNDAMENTALS: FREEDOM, INDEPENDENCE, AND LETTING CHILDREN BE CHILDREN

I t wasn't long after my initial idea of writing this book that I was invited to a dinner party. Ashley, an American, along with her Dutch husband lives in the centre of Amsterdam with their three children. Ashley had invited several women, both Dutch and expats, over for the evening. We sat around her living room, munching on sushi and skipping from one topic to the next, when the conversation focused on Ashley's stunning home.

The home, a historic canal house, was spread over several floors and was connected by a series of treacherously steep stairs. (The Dutch are known for such stairs, a result of 16th- and 17th-century buildings being taxed on their width. Hence, to save money, houses were built with narrow and sometimes extremely steep stairs!)

A newly-minted American "Amsterdammer" pressed Ashley on the issue: Had it not been a consideration in her decision to buy the home? Had she ever fallen? Had the children ever been injured?

Ashley chuckled while saying that, miraculously, her whole family had indeed lived to see another day and that her four-year-old actually used the 2nd-storey open set of stairs as a jungle gym. She laughed and said that her home would "give any American baby-proofer a heart attack. They would probably suggest tearing the entire home down. They wouldn't even know where to begin."

The other three Dutch mothers in the room looked on with blank faces. "*What* on earth is a 'baby-proofer'?" one named Eline exclaimed. A bubbly American from San Francisco jumped in, explaining that it's somewhat common to have a professional come into your home and inspect it for baby safety (or this could be done on your own). "And this is required by law?" Charlijn asked. "Well, no,"

178

the other explained, "but it's for your child's safety." Eline wasn't hearing any of it. "You even pay for this!?" she questioned. A heated conversation erupted in the corner of the room with the three Dutch mothers having a good laugh at this "very American" type of behaviour. Eline still looked confused as Ashley explained, "It's not mandatory, it's just cultural."

Cultural, indeed—as was the current exchange taking place between the Dutch and American mothers. The Americans felt the need to somehow explain and/ or justify such behaviours, whereas the Dutch were keen to keep the joke going. *(I thought of my own Amsterdam apartment with its baby-proofed electric sockets and pillowed sharp-edges with a pang of embarrassment. Where did I get those ideas? It certainly was never mentioned to me by any Dutch person, nor anything I saw in their homes.)*

The conversation inevitably turned to the open fireplace in the centre of the living room. Ashley matter-of-factly continued, "for instance, a 'baby-proofer' would have likely suggested placing a screen or a glass panel in front of the fireplace." Miriam, a Dutch woman in her late forties, dramatically took a swig of her wine and commanded the attention of the room. "Look, you want to know how the Dutch would 'baby-proof' that fireplace? When your kids are babies or maybe one year old, you move them away from the fireplace and tell them, 'Watch out, be careful, it's hot!'" She continued, all eyes on her, "And when they are two or three, you say, 'Hey Sanne, you want to play with the fire? Okay, fine. Stick your hand in it!' They do, they scream—and then … the fireplace is 'baby proofed'! Trust me, they'll never stick their hands in there again. They're smart like little adults, and need to learn these things for themselves!" The room erupted in laughter. The expats who have been here the longest smiled knowingly. This is indeed not a flippant joke but instead quite close to the truth. The others, having only lived in Amsterdam for a short while, laughed as well, but clearly thought that the statement was absurd and could have only been a joke … and perhaps, after all, this Miriam woman had had one too many glasses of wine.

What is certain is that none of us North Americans, myself included, are ready to let our children thrust their hands into an open fire. Yet Miriam's final remarks highlight a fundamental pillar of Dutch parenting: children should be given the freedom to independently learn, fail, discover, and explore in the ever-important process of growing up.

Let's take a closer look at this notion of "freedom" and other key elements of Dutch parenting:

In this chapter

- Freedom
- Independence
- No Dutch helicopters
- Letting children be children

Wild and free

The belief in freedom and independence is a fundamental principle in Dutch parenting. As the Dutch expression goes, "*Een kind opvoeden is een kind loslaten*," which roughly translates to the notion that to raise a child is to let a child go. When I asked several Dutch parents to describe, in one sentence, the essence of Dutch parenting, this expression popped up more than any other. As one Dutch father told me, "The most important lesson I learned about raising children, was actually that you must first let them go." Not surprisingly, Dutch parents highly value these notions of freedom, autonomy, and independence when raising children.

There isn't a specific moment when Dutch parents decide to consciously give their children more independence or freedom, as this behaviour is actually carried out from birth. Dutch babies and toddlers are given the space and time to cultivate their "independent lives"—whether this is by getting used to sleeping in their own bed or playing in their own space or spending quality time alone in their playpen (*babybox*).

Cultural perceptions of "letting go"

Within my North American circles, a similar notion of the Dutch "letting go" attitude in parenting had never arisen. These mothers also wanted independent, self-sufficient children, but they certainly were not comfortable with the idea of "letting go." In fact, when I pressed them on the subject, many of the "Anglo" mothers I spoke with had strong negative connotations with the idea and equated it to older children going to college or moving out of the family home. The association was certainly not a positive one and the idea of "letting go" of small children was seen more as an act of poor parenting or negligence.

Dutch parenting has often been described as laid-back, relaxed, and quite permissive. While I wouldn't argue with any of these observations, I think one could make the wrong assumption that this parenting style is without substance or reasoning. Dutch parents are usually highly involved in their children's lives and play a very active role. Their attitude may be more casual than other nations, such as America or Canada, but this comes from a deeply ingrained believe in the importance of autonomy.

I cannot count how many times I have heard foreigners (expats and tourists) complain about Dutch children and their behaviour. Dutch parents do appear to be rather "hands-off" and quite content to let "children be children," something which can irk or confuse parents from other cultures.

Thoughts on "Dutch-style" parenting

"I'm pretty sure the majority of American parents would classify Dutch parenting as some sort of 'free-range' parenting. It's not that it's a bad thing—I have come to appreciate many aspects of it—however, it is very different than what we know!"

American mom (living in NL)

Dutch mom

"I think Dutch parents are more easy-going, but the Netherlands is a lot safer than America. And less competitive. Which gives you more freedom to let go and not worry too much. Although I feel it is changing a bit towards the American style. Especially with parents that have big careers."

Dutch mom

"I think the Dutch let their kids be a little looser than Americans. I, of course, believe boundaries have to be given, but you can find a balance of boundaries and independence."

American mom (living in NL)

"If I'm honest, I find the Dutch approach of just ignoring the children—including bad or mean behavior—pretty uncomfortable. I always interject if I see my child doing something inappropriate or being unsafe or unkind. I still can't figure out if Dutch parents are just uninterested or if they have an actual philosophy that guides their parenting."

American mom (living in NL)

"Dutch parenting (from what I have seen) can be too free—our neighbour's two-year old boy that was lost for 30 minutes in Amsterdam. He had walked down to the end of the street, crossed an extremely busy road to the other side where there was a canal… thankfully there was a conscientious citizen that stayed with him until my husband found him. This family might have been a bit of an exception in allowing their kids too much freedom at too young an age, but I have seen a lot of Dutch parents who give 'too much' freedom."

"There is definitely a different style to parenting here (in the Netherlands) than in the U.K. I've noticed, especially at the playgrounds, that Dutch parents are much more 'hands off.' They don't step in to actively discipline when children are arguing or bothering each other. I've had a hard time getting used to this. I will admit I'm concerned if my children will adjust back to the 'British way' when we move back."

British mom (living in NL)

Different cultures, different values

When comparing the values of parents around the globe, it is fascinating to see that different cultures have very different ideas on what matters most when raising their children. Sara Harkness and her colleagues have, in their research on parenting in a cultural context, highlighted the different values which parents hold. For instance:

- ✔ Italian parents value social and emotional abilities and an even temperament
- ✔ Spanish parents value highly sociable children
- ✔ Swedish parents value security and happiness
- ✔ American parents value intellectual ability

Not surprisingly, their research found that Dutch parents valued **independence, long attention spans, and predictable schedules** most.

Nary a helicopter in sight

When Kaia was 8 months old I stumbled upon a new park in our area, run by a local volunteer parent association. The playground was a familiar Dutch scene —the children happily played together, ran, screamed, occasionally fought and/or cried while their mothers and fathers gathered together, backs to their children, drinking coffee, deep in adult discussions.

You will be hard pressed to find the North-American style "helicopter parenting" on a typical Dutch playground. The term "helicopter parenting" emerged in Canada and the United States in the past decade to describe parents who pay extremely close attention to their child's activities and experiences, tending to hover over their child's every move. At the numerous playgrounds I have frequented with Kaia, the exact opposite tends to be true—nary a helicopter in sight.

I will never forget the sheer look of panic on a mother's face who ran up to me, her eldest daughter in hand, at Kaia's favourite neighbourhood playground. She asked, breathlessly, if I had seen a small boy in a red jacket. I said no and offered to help her search. Luckily two long minutes later, we found her son, a block from the playground, squatting next to a canal quietly playing with his toy car. As we walked back to the park she sternly lectured him on the importance of staying within the playground's gates. The sun was shining (a bit of a rarity) and what happened next truly left me scratching my head. As they re-entered the playground the son headed for the sandbox, the daughter for the swings, and the mother for the crowded bench of parents. This wouldn't have been unusual apart from the fact that this particular bench was completely out of sight of the children playing near the inviting exit. The Dutch parents (including the mother whose child had just been
188

missing) casually chatted away, facing the sun, backs to their children. The previous
dramatic incident, which still had my heart racing, was seemingly forgotten.
The Dutch children played, the Dutch parents chatted and laughed... and I? I sat,
continually scanning the playground for any more escape attempts, one eye on the
gate, and the other on the children.

Dutch playgrounds are in stark contrast to the playgrounds I've frequented
on our holiday trips to Canada and America, where I've witnessed fully grown
adults attempting to squeeze themselves down child-sized slides or awkwardly
climb play structures while tightly holding their children's hands the whole
time. For all the countless hours spent in Dutch playgrounds, I have never once
observed a Dutch parent hovering over a child in a similar fashion. Would the
"helicopter-parent" trend ever cross the Atlantic and swoop Dutch parents up in
its overprotective arms? I seriously doubt it!

Dutch moms don't hover

Dutch mom

"What-on-earth does "helicopter parenting" even mean? Yeah, I know, I'm very Dutch indeed…"

"I love how Dutch parents give kids space to explore, fall down, and pick themselves up. I rarely see highly strung or anxious Dutch parents and I'm sure it makes for more relaxed, confident, and happy children."

British mom (living in NL)

"I believe American parents hover too much. I want to be more Dutch in this respect. I think it's important to let children discover who they are and what they can do, even though it can be painful at times."

American mom (living in NL)

Hungarian mom (living in NL)

"By Dutch standards I am considered overprotective and controlling. I'm trying to take more of a Dutch approach, but it is hard!"

"Dutch parents are very laid back—especially on the playground. This is a generalization, but I've found it to be true. Of course, I would also add that American parents are constantly monitoring their children and overly obsessed with manners and not 'offending' others—which is the other extreme."

American mom (living in NL)

"I am American but would definitely not describe myself as a 'helicopter parent.' I'm pretty relaxed and like to let my kids just play on their own with minimal involvement from me."

American mom

"A lot of Dutch parents believe that children should sort out their own issues. This means allowing them to have little arguments or fights so that they learn to manage those situations (of course, I do not mean physical fights)."

Dutch mom

Letting children be children

Dutch parents do not believe in pushing their children too hard. In general, Dutch children have less homework than American children and undertake fewer extra-curricular activities. Dutch parents also are less consumed by the academic achievements of their children, and often have a rather casual or laid-back attitude towards the notion of success.

In my own experience, I have observed "helicopter parenting" to often coincide with a competitive attitude, geared towards the quest for successful children—something rarely exhibited by Dutch parents. Speaking with an Australian friend about her daughter's start at school, it seems that the competitive nature of North American parents has sadly made its way "down-under."

"Do you know that over half the class could already read when Emma started school? Half the class—and most of them aren't even four yet!! And you know what?" she continued, outraged, "there are no kids outside our house after school. None. No one is playing in the big backyards or running down the streets. They are all inside. Inside being coached and tutored on how to bloody read!"

"Do you remember our parents teaching us to read?" she asked.

I didn't. In fact, when she spoke of running down the streets, my own childhood memories of playing hide and seek down muddy back lanes and bumpy front streets were the only thing to enter my mind. No flashcards, no coached play, no structured reading lessons.

"It's exhausting" my Australian working-mother friend continued. "I battle with myself all the time. On the one hand I just want them to be outside to play and

enjoy their childhood, and on the other hand it kills me to learn that all the other kids could read better than Emma. I have to remind myself she's only four, and that they are the crazy ones with their workbooks on a summer's day, but it can play tricks on your mind."

Often described as "concerted cultivation," there appears to be a new wave of parenting spreading across the Anglo countries—from Australia, to North America and the U.K.—fraught with flashcards, early language development, music and "sensory play" classes. The name of the game appears to be stimulation, development, and achievement.

According to an article on the popular U.S. website Jezebel, American parents are highly focused on "making sure that their children's talents are groomed for success." In the article, "Parenting: Are You Doing It Right? Depends on Where You Live," they cite research from our favourite (and previously mentioned) Sara Harkness and Charles Super to compare the attitudes of Dutch parents versus Americans.

"Nearly 25 percent of all of the descriptors used by American parents were a derivation of smart, gifted or advanced. In the Netherlands, meanwhile, parents used 'smart' to describe their children only 10 percent of the time."

Let's hope Dutch parents remain immune to the negative influences of "helicopter parenting" and continue to allow their children to, well, just be children!

What can we learn from Dutch moms

American mom (living in NL)

"I love how things are much less competitive here between parents, kids, sports teams, etc.—in the U.S. it can get really nasty!"

"I am a Dutch woman living with two kids in America. As for the American attitude towards parenting, I think it's part 'keeping up with the Joneses' and part 'we are the greatest.' If you constantly feel you have to live up to some sort of imaginary and non-arbitrary standard, you can get pretty anxious and stressed."

Dutch mom (living in America)

American mom

"As an American, married to a Dutch man, it has been interesting. We live in the USA, in California, which is filled with helicopter parents who question and compare everything!"

"As a cloggie, working and living in the U.K. it often makes me cringe to hear parents going on about being worried about what others may or may not think of them. Who gives a banana! Be yourself and be proud of it! The Dutch way of seeing things is: 'What you see is what you get. Don't like what you see? Turn around and walk.'"

Dutch mom

Dutch mom

"I read a number of American blogs and I find the mommy-war discourse at times horrifying, and I wonder how parental anxiety levels in the U.S. got so high!"

Dutch mom (living in America)

"I will never forget the moment that we were at an American school and the teacher started reading all the results of the tests of our 4th grader. At the end of her list she asked us if we had any questions and I said, 'Yes!' I asked her: 'Is my daughter a happy person in your lessons?' The teacher definitely did not see that question coming, and I told her that I didn't care and was not interested in her results, I only cared if she was happy, because in my opinion (and according to her results) they will only learn a lot when they are happy."

CHAPTER 9

DUTCH MOMS
FEEL LESS GUILT

During my four years as a mother, it has been a fascinating ride observing the different cultural norms and behaviours associated with motherhood in the Lowlands. Barely out of the "new-mother" gate, it became clear to me that Dutch mothers were different—in many ways—to the North American archetype I was used to.

In the first year, I struggled with difficult decisions regarding breast-feeding (To stop or not?), returning to work (How can I abandon my baby?), and daycare (Am I a bad mother?). I noticed one striking difference between myself and the Dutch mothers around me: guilt. Or rather, a lack of it!

The bottom line is Dutch mothers don't feel as guilty as North American mothers—and that's a good thing. I am not saying that Dutch mothers do not feel any guilt whatsoever, because unfortunately some level of guilt is part and parcel of being a mother, no matter where you live. I do, however, believe that Dutch mothers feel less guilt than their North American counterparts. This healthy attitude allows them to achieve a much more balanced approach to motherhood and its demands. In a Maclean's magazine article "How Dutch women got to be the happiest in the world," the author states:

> *"Dutch women have smashed the vicious circle of guilt that traps other Western women, to embrace a progressive form of work-life balance."*

Let's investigate further the concept of guilt in motherhood, and how Dutch moms have a healthy outlook on their children and their role and responsibility as mothers.

Back to work

Most working mothers in the Netherlands put their children in crèche at the age of three months. This is the standard, as explained in Chapter 5, as Dutch maternity leave normally ends three months after birth. Of course, some working mothers tack on additional holiday time or leave but it is rare to see many taking a leave of longer than four to five months.

For both of my children, I opted for a leave of 7.5 months. I felt this was an acceptable compromise between the generous Canadian one-year leave, and the Dutch dismal three-month leave. The reaction to my decision, on either side of the Atlantic, could not have been more different! My Canadian friends and relatives all felt deeply sorry for me: "Only 7.5 months? How are you going to manage? What kind of country do you live in? How is that even possible? The baby and I weren't even sleeping through the night yet?!" The Dutch reactions, however, were on the complete opposite end of the spectrum and ranged from surprise to incredulity: "How can you afford that? What does your husband do for a living? Why would you want to??"

Of all the comments, the latter caught me most by surprise. "*Why would you want to?*" The truth was, it was never said in a heartless way. These were loving, caring, working Dutch mothers, who truthfully wanted to know and understand my reason for taking a longer leave. Most knew the Dutch three-month *zwangerschapsverlof* was a standard practice, a given, and did not question whether it was right or wrong. Never in our discussions did I ever hear an ounce of guilt surrounding the topic of returning to work. Of course, some mothers wished it was different and that they could spend more time with their babies, but accepted that it was not to be. Some even stated outright and without shame, that they were happy to go back to work and have routine, structure and fulfilment back in their lives. Both camps simply accepted the reality and got on with it. I do believe this relatively guilt-free attitude towards work is primarily due to the fact that many Dutch mothers have the option of returning to work on a part-time basis, allowing them a perfect balance between "working-mom" as well as "stay-at-home-mom."

Guilt? What guilt?

Dutch mom

"Guilt???? LOL! WTF is that?!"

Dutch mom (living in America)

"As a Dutch mother living in NY, I have not felt guilty for returning to part time work seven months after giving birth. Everyone makes their decision based on their situation. I do know that for many mothers this is not an option, so I feel privileged to be able to have a choice and not feel guilty."

Dutch mom

"We do have doubt and guilt, but probably because of the pragmatic attitude inherent in our culture we also simply just accept; c'est la vie, que sera sera."

"I remember my Dutch co-workers saying two things: they had to go back to work because they needed the money to pay the bills. Secondly, they were glad to be at work so they could recover from their hectic home and be able to socialise."

American mom (living in NL)

"I don't think the Dutch are less guilty I think they are just more 'followers.' The consultatiebureau tells you how to raise your child and everyone just does as they are told. I myself have no guilt. I do as a mom what I feel is right and that's guilt-free!"

South African mom (living in NL)

"I am a Dutch woman who had her first two daughters in the Netherlands and my youngest in Sweden where I have lived since 2008. Here in Scandinavia, they are even more relaxed. There is no pressure to go back to work so soon. Also the employers fully understand that if your child is sick that you as a mother stay home a few days. There is even a 'social insurance bank' to pay those 'lost' days to the mother. In Holland we had to take a holiday when the child was sick…. or have grandmothers jump in…. or simply lie and say we are sick ourselves to prevent spending all our holiday pay. Also the maternity leave should be a bit longer. Like six months. That would be much better. Personally I find a year a bit long to stay away from work."

Dutch mom

"I'm a Dutch mother and I do get plagued by guilt all the time. I'm a stay-at-home mom and I believe it takes a village to raise a child, but during the day, on my own, I can't be that village, which makes me feel guilty."

Dutch mom

Dutch mom

"I was raised in America by a Dutch mother who lived in Holland during WWII. She learned to be practical and do what was best for the family and not what everyone around her thought and expected. I applied this to my life and passed it onto my kids. No guilt feelings here!"

"I've spent the last 12 years fighting against the 'guilt' that we get here in the USA. I'm balanced with the attitudes of my Dutch husband. It's a difficult balance to achieve, but I think I got it. I stopped defending myself, and I let go of guilt... It wasn't healthy for me or my kids!"

American mom

Breast or bottle

The attitude I encountered towards breastfeeding also had a guilt-free component. My Dutch midwives, friends, and colleagues all shared a common belief: of course breastfeeding was beneficial for the baby, but it was also not meant for everyone. Again, this was a rather freeing thought. It removed all notions of guilt and self-blame from the equation. Formula was not seen as a lesser substitute, but rather, for some, a practical and necessary solution.

I was told by my Dutch *kraamzorg*, doctor, and midwife that it was "just as good" as breast-milk (a claim which I do not fully agree with) and that the decision to breastfeed or not, should take into account all factors such as the mother's health, mental state, family life, working life, sleeping situation, husband's support, and so on. Something I *do* agree with.

After the birth of my daughter, when I was first struggling with breastfeeding, sleeplessness, and exhaustion, my Dutch midwife sat me down and matter-of-factly said, "Colleen, it's just like being on an airplane. You must put on your air mask first before the baby's. A healthy, happy mother is much more important than which milk your baby drinks."

Breastfeeding eventually worked out fine for me, but when I did stop after an exhausting month back at work, I tried to adopt the no-guilt attitude of my Dutch friends and colleagues. Of course, being a Canadian, there was still a small, remaining element of guilt, but I tried to adopt a pragmatic Dutch approach.

This would be the first, of many times, I would also hear the "oxygen-mask-first" adage in relation to motherhood. A simple yet effective comparison rooted in traditional Dutch pragmatism. As I left the hospital with my second child, my Dutch maternity nurse repeated the phrase, this time with an added caveat: "Take care of yourself first—and feel no guilt in the process."

Dutch mom

"I'm Dutch and stayed home with my daughter until she was one year old, because I wanted to, not because of guilt. She was bottle fed because it is more practical, and I was raised using Dutch common sense."

"Maybe some feel guilt, and some don't. One thing pragmatists don't do is get hung up and overthink stuff to the point where they don't know if they are coming or going. And most Dutch people I know are pragmatic."

Dutch mom

British mom (living in NL)

"I'm a Brit living in Friesland. The mums here are so tough it's a wonder to behold. No guilt. Not ever. I have learned so much from them living here in the Netherlands."

Children are not necessarily a reflection of their parents

What I personally find most interesting about Dutch parents is their ability to separate their children's talents (or lack thereof) from their own. I will never forget the first time I encountered this attitude, as it took me slightly aback. I had just been introduced to a new work colleague. We were having coffee and she was telling me about her life and family. She went on to describe her children. When it came to her daughter, she paused. "She's very bright. Possibly too bright." And her son? "Well, he's very sweet, but not the smartest kid. He'll do just fine though, as he's a little charmer." 'Not the smartest,' had I just heard that correctly? It wasn't often you heard parents discuss their children in such an open and honest way!

The beauty is that Dutch parents are able to separate themselves from their children. Their children are not necessarily a reflection of themselves—nor every good or bad thing they have ever done. They are simply autonomous beings, with individual characters, strengths, and weaknesses. It's an utterly refreshing perspective as it automatically removes guilt from the core of the parenting equation. Little Johnny is *shite* at math? Not your fault! Little Sarah seems to be a bit of a brat these days? Maybe hormones, puberty, or a character flaw? Choose one of the above, or all three, as none directly relates to you! All joking aside, it's a much healthier way of looking at your child, faults and all. It also frees parents from too much praise or too much criticism for their children's strengths or weaknesses.

"The biggest difference that I've noticed is that it seems that American parents feel themselves responsible for their children's continuous, all-encompassing happiness and wellbeing. Whereas, as a Dutch, I feel responsible only to raise my children to become independent, self-reliant, responsible adults with as many tools as I can give them."

Dutch mom

Dutch/ Australian mom

"I am a mother with Dutch heritage with my Dutch mother living close by me in Australia. I remember feeling somewhat guilty about not feeling guilty. Everybody around me seemed to be agonizing and stressed about everything! Sleep, nappies/diapers, breastfeeding, coming into parental bed, crying or not, when to eat solids. And it didn't let up all the way through to high school! The rare occasion I did buy into something, my mother, in Dutch, would say (in polite translation), 'What in the world are you DOING?' And that would be that."

American mom

"We love feeling guilty in America! Otherwise you're not a good mother!"

"Weirdly enough, as a Dutch mom in the U.S., I'm experiencing this guilt-phenomenon in reverse. I went into motherhood with my Dutch mind-set, but the constant questioning of that method often did make me feel guilt. And then a little rebellious! At some point, when my son was still a baby, I would always be asked the same question if I was out and about without him. (which we all know is hardly ever!) First thing people would say was 'where's the baby?!' (On a date night…in a bar!) My standard answer to that became 'oh I left him in the car, but don't worry, I cracked open a window.'"

Dutch mom (living in America)

Has all this guiltless happiness rubbed off on me? I'd like to think so. I work four days a week, and have managed to banish all guilt surrounding this decision. I love my children, I love what I do, and I've learnt from the other Dutch moms around me that there is no "one-size-fits-all" approach to motherhood. Dutch women rarely compare themselves to each other. You hear neither self-praise nor self-doubt in relation to their personal parenting decisions. This attitude is truly refreshing and freeing – and something that could be adopted my moms around the world!

CONCLUSION

During my four years as a mother, I have had the privilege of observing firsthand the values, beliefs, and systems surrounding motherhood in the Netherlands. Early in the process, I realized that if I was going to embark on the journey of parenthood in the Netherlands, I'd need to throw all my preconceived notions out the window and open my mind to doing things a completely different way—the Dutch way, that is! Living in a foreign country forces you outside your comfort zone on a daily basis. Add having a baby to the mix, and you'll end up discovering more about your host country—and yourself—than you ever thought possible.

Coming from a place of genuine curiosity and intrigue, I've learned more about the Dutch maternity system and their "culture of motherhood" than, dare I say, about my own country. Whether it was the highly personalised midwifery care, the practical details on how to prepare for giving birth in one's own bed, the "right way" to comfort a crying baby in the middle of the night, or how to just "let go" as a parent, I've closely observed how the Netherlands' prevailing values of freedom, independence, and egalitarianism have truly influenced all levels and domains of Dutch society—including that of motherhood.

As an outsider looking in, I truly believe Dutch mothers come pretty close to "having it all." The Netherlands' flexible work policies have allowed Dutch moms to master the ever-elusive work–life balance. Whether it be the ability to work part-time or the freedom for Dutch fathers to take a "daddy day," the fundamentals of Dutch work culture hugely benefit all families—especially those with small children. Although maternity leave is not nearly long enough, the acceptance of part-time work (even at a senior level) allows many women to not have to make the exceedingly difficult decision between being either a "stay-at-home mom" or a "working mom." Dutch mothers do not have to attempt to squeeze their busy lives and careers into a rigid archaic system, but instead have the liberty of finding a balance that works for them as individuals.

Although many Dutch mothers nowadays are not familiar with the 3 R's, these guiding principles are still very much a part of the fundamentals of Dutch parenting. Whether or not they know the trio by name seems of little relevance, as the vast majority of Dutch mothers follow fairly straight-forward routines and schedules. I would argue that these routines result in a certain level of predictability that better allows for children to thrive. Research has shown that, as a direct result of this, Dutch babies and children sleep better, have less "sleep-related issues," and not surprisingly, are happier as a result. We all know that having children who do not sleep well can significantly impact a parent's overall health and happiness. It will therefore come as no surprise that well-rested parents make for happier parents as well!

Parenting in the Netherlands is often described by foreigners as overly liberal and permissive. There is, however, "method to the madness," as the notably laid-back attitudes of Dutch parents are firmly rooted in the belief that a child's independence and autonomy should be respected and allowed to flourish. Dutch parents are also significantly less consumed by their children's achievements. This healthy attitude allows Dutch mothers—and fathers— to separate their children's accomplishments from that of their own. This refreshing perspective leads to less competitive behavior and ultimately aides in removing superfluous guilt from the core of the parenting equation.

Over the past few years, studies have been published proclaiming that Dutch children are the happiest in the world. Many have tried to analyze and distill these results, searching for the "holy grail" of universal parental wisdom. How did Dutch children get to be so happy? Was it their rather laid-back upbringing? Their parents' adherence to routine? Their liberated childhoods? The Dutch educational system? Or all of the above? How can we replicate this happiness, bottle it up, and export it to other nations? As we can't all hop on a plane and move to the Netherlands to raise our children, can we ensure that our children will be on the right track for this type of happiness?

The answer to all of the above questions is actually alarmingly simple—and if you take away one thing from this book, let it be this—happier mothers make for happier children. We may not all have the luxuries (yes luxuries!) afforded to Dutch mothers and fathers, but we are now armed with the basic knowledge— and proof—that parental contentment has a profound effect on children.

Dutch parenting is a refreshing combination of old-fashioned practical beliefs and modern-day thinking. Whether you live in Europe, North America, Asia, or beyond, I urge you to consider applying a lesson or two from the "Dutch style" of parenting and see whether it brings greater simplicity and balance to your own life. The ultimate secret from observing Dutch moms in the Netherlands is that there is no "one-size-fits-all" to motherhood and that finding balance in your life will lead to greater happiness for both you and your children!

About Us

About the Author

Colleen Geske is the blogger and best-selling author behind the hugely popular '*Stuff Dutch People Like*' brand. Originally from Winnipeg, Canada, Colleen has called Amsterdam her home since 2004. Described as "blunt, provocative and wickedly funny", her blog and books offer an often satirical look at Dutch culture as seen through the eyes of an outsider.

About Stuff Dutch People Like

Stuff Dutch People Like is a celebration of all things Dutch. Started as a simple blog back in 2011, the Stuff Dutch People Like community now boasts a loyal following of over a half million fans in the Netherlands and around the world! The original Stuff Dutch People Like book was published in 2013 and became an instant international bestseller, with other books following suit! Visit us at www.stuffdutchpeoplelike.com

Stuff Dutch People Like *(The Original)*

"Blunt, provocative and wickedly funny", *Stuff Dutch People Like* is a satirical look at Dutch culture as seen through the eyes of an outsider. From *Appelmoes* to *Zwarte Piet* and everything in between, *Stuff Dutch People Like* covers it all—and then some!

Stuff Dutch People Say

From the creators of *Stuff Dutch People Like* comes this hilarious companion. *Stuff Dutch People Say* delves deep into the linguistic world of the Lowlands, exploring what happens when Dutch and English collide. From funny Dutch words, incomprehensible Dutch expressions and hysterical examples of Dunglish, we've got you covered!

Stuff Dutch People Eat

Stuff Dutch People Eat is a comprehensive celebration of Dutch cuisine. Whether you're looking for festive sweets, traditional tastes or colonial classics, we've got something for every appetite! From breakfast straight through to dessert, *Stuff Dutch People Eat* will lead you through a culinary adventure spanning flavours— and centuries! Discover 40 easy-to-make recipes that are sure to restore your faith in the delightfully delicious Dutch kitchen! *Eet smakelijk*!

Stuff Dutch Moms Like

Stuff Dutch Moms Like investigates why Dutch moms are amongst the happiest in the world—and how they manage to have it all! Filled with hilarious anecdotes, tips and tricks, *Stuff Dutch Moms Like* takes an inside look at parenting in the Netherlands and the secrets to raising the happiest children in the world!

Photo Sources/Credits

Page	Attribution		
6/7	Catherine		
13	David Spreekmeester		
37	Stefanie Archer Photography	www.stefaniearcher.nl	
42	Jason Lander	https://www.flickr.com/photos/eyeliam/7353085948/	
49	Jason Lander	https://www.flickr.com/photos/eyeliam/7168299649	CC BY 2.0
54	Jason Lander	https://www.flickr.com/photos/eyeliam/7353570920	CC BY 2.0
63	Jason Lander	https://www.flickr.com/photos/eyeliam/7168298937	CC BY 2.0
74	Luca Nebuloni	https://www.flickr.com/photos/nebulux/9825568964/	CC BY 2.0
82/83	Irene van der Meijs	Shutterstock	
85	Alexander Baxevanis	https://www.flickr.com/photos/futureshape/5052466404/	CC BY 2.0
89	105MM		
106	Chris Macks	https://www.flickr.com/photos/65704572@N04/6201687491/	CC BY 2.0
125	FaceMePLS	https://www.flickr.com/photos/faceme/14518924032/	CC BY 2.0
131	Stefanie Archer Photography	www.stefaniearcher.nl	
136/137	Peter Eijking		
139	Marco Spaapen	https://www.flickr.com/photos/marcusspaapen/6871186102/	CC BY 2.0
143	faungg's photos	https://www.flickr.com/photos/44534236@N00/5899089233/	CC BY-ND 2.0
148	Scott & Elaine van der Chijs	https://www.flickr.com/photos/scottvanderchijs/4729943439	CC BY 2.0
163	Stefanie Archer Photog.	www.stefaniearcher.nl	
167	Stefanie Archer Photog.	www.stefaniearcher.nl	
174	Donnie Ray Jones	https://www.flickr.com/photos/donnieray/14276228510/	CC BY 2.0
186/187	105MM		
197	Boudewijn Berends	https://www.flickr.com/photos/boudewijnberends/4745425727/	CC BY 2.0
213	Rudi Wells Fotografie		
214	Pim Ras		